In "Disrupting and Design Thinking Education", Dr. Meadows paints a broad landscape of learning systems transformed by innovators and technology. Dive in to find a range of breakthrough ideas.

Gary A. Bolles, author of "The Next Rules of Work" | Chair for the Future of Work for Singularity University | Co-Founder, eParachute.com | 1.5 million LinkedIn Learners

This is an essential and timely book on the need to re-design education – full of innovative ideas on how to compete in the new economy of AI-enabled learning and work. Full of insightful ideas and innovative recommendations, this work provides students, educators, investors, and employers with a solid foundation and path forward for adapting to and thriving in the digital economy. Employees will need to continuously up-skill; every job will be redefined; and education methodologies will need to be re-created for the future. This book is essential reading!

Paul W. Bradley, Chairman and CEO, Caprica International | Member, B20 Task Force on the Future of Work and Education for the G20

A must-read for every learner, parent, educator, and educational investor – in schools and corporate L&D! Whether you're crafting your own educational journey or providing one to others, you'll need this book's vision of education's future and tech-enabled (not driven) approach to create it.

Professor Virginia Cha, Global Agenda Council Member, World Economic Forum | Academic Director, SMART Innovation Academy (Singapore MIT Alliance for Research and Technology)

AI is enabling a radical new future of work, and we need to learn in equally new ways. This book provides essential advice for how to envision the new world of learning and how to create it.

Dr. Chris Marshall, VP – Artificial Intelligence and Data Analytics, IDC Asia Pacific

The future of learning is mobile, applied, social, and integrated with a new landscape of work. We need to redesign learning and digitally transform it, just as we're digitally transforming our enterprises. Here you'll find the needs we must serve, new business models for viability, and enabling technologies, so you can lead transformation with confidence.

So-Young Kang, Chairman, AwakenFutures | Founder and CEO, Gnowbe | WEF Young Global Leader

Disrupting and Design Thinking Education

Meadows proposes an approach to the education business that begins with needs, and proposes educational and business models, supported by new technologies.

This book takes a design-thinking and disruption perspective on the future of education. Beginning with shocking statistics on cost, time, and lengthy debt repayment, it presents a clear case for disruption in the education sector. It continues by examining future skills in the age of AI, machine learning, and robotics. In this new age, businesses need a new kind of workforce, and workers need to equip themselves to survive and thrive. Drawing upon tools and techniques from disruption and design-thinking, Meadows puts forward new frameworks of education, business, and technology – all with examples of educators (and learners) already doing it today.

This book provides rigorous thinking and practical guidance for professionals in the education industry and budding education entrepreneurs, as well as homeschooling parents.

Dr. CJ Meadows leads an Innovation and Entrepreneurship Center at S P Jain School of Global Management, working at the intersection of IT, business strategy, and design. She has a DBA-IT from Harvard Business School and 25+ years' experience globally as an Accenture consultant and entrepreneur.

Routledge-Solaris Focus on Strategy, Wisdom and Skill

The Series is advised and edited by Charles Chao Rong Phua, the Chairman of the Solaris Consortium of Management Consultancies.

Pragmatism in Foreign Policy
Comparing the US, China, and Singapore
Charles Chao Rong Phua

Cultural Pragmatism for US-China Relations
Breaking the Gridlock and Co-Creating Our Future
Charles Chao Rong Phua

Policy Strategy and Innovation Primer
Process, Praxis and Tools
Charles Chao Rong Phua

The Principles of Policy Thought
A Philosophical Approach to Public Policy
Hae Young Lee

Disrupting and Design Thinking Education
New Technology, Designs, and Business Models
Dr. CJ Meadows

Disrupting and Design Thinking Education

New Technology, Designs, and Business Models

Dr. CJ Meadows

LONDON AND NEW YORK

First published 2025
by Routledge
4 Park Square, Milton Park, Abingdon, Oxon OX14 4RN

and by Routledge
605 Third Avenue, New York, NY 10158

Routledge is an imprint of the Taylor & Francis Group, an informa business

British Library Cataloguing-in-Publication Data
A catalogue record for this book is available from the British Library

Library of Congress Cataloging-in-Publication Data
Names: Meadows, C. J. (Carolyn Jean), author.
Title: Disrupting and design thinking education: new technology, designs, and business models / CJ Meadows.
Description: Abingdon, Oxon; New York, NY: Routledge, 2025. |
Series: Routledge-Solaris focus on strategy, wisdom and skill |
Includes bibliographical references and index. |
Summary: "Meadows proposes an approach to the education business that begins with needs, and proposes educational and business models, supported by new technologies. This book takes a design-thinking and disruption perspective on the future of education. Beginning with shocking statistics on cost, time, and lengthy debt repayment, it presents a clear case for disruption in the education sector. It continues by examining future skills in the age of AI, machine learning, and robotics. In this new age, businesses need a new kind of workforce, and workers need to equip themselves to survive and thrive. Drawing upon tools and techniques from disruption and design-thinking, Meadows puts forward new frameworks of education, business, and technology – all with examples of educators (and learners) already doing it today. This book provides rigorous thinking and practical guidance for professionals in the education industry and budding education entrepreneurs, as well as homeschooling parents"– Provided by publisher.
Identifiers: LCCN 2024030593 (print) | LCCN 2024030594 (ebook) |
ISBN 9781032375427 (hardback) | ISBN 9781032375434 (paperback) |
ISBN 9781003340713 (ebook)
Subjects: LCSH: Educational planning. | Education–Effect of technological innovations on. | Business and education. | Education–Economic aspects. |
Labor supply–Effect of education on.
Classification: LCC LC71.2 .M43 2025 (print) | LCC LC71.2 (ebook) |
DDC 371.2/07–dc23/eng/20240730
LC record available at https://lccn.loc.gov/2024030593
LC ebook record available at https://lccn.loc.gov/2024030594

ISBN: 978-1-032-37542-7 (hbk)
ISBN: 978-1-032-37543-4 (pbk)
ISBN: 978-1-003-34071-3 (ebk)

DOI: 10.4324/9781003340713

Typeset in Times New Roman
by Deanta Global Publishing Services, Chennai, India

Contents

Acknowledgments

God, family, business and community, then me. Those are pretty clear priorities that have always served me well. So, my first thanks is a reflection of how I write. I pray beforehand to be a voice for God's inspiration and empowerment, then write down what He gives me. Thank you, God, for giving me so much, for others and for myself.

Thank you, husband Chris and kids Jonathan, Anna, David, and Sarah Marshall. I know you're now 19, 19, 21, and 22, but you'll always be my kids. You're patient with me and probably thankful I always have writing to do, so I keep out of your hair. Just letting you know I'm on to that little trick. I suspect you've paid my publishers to keep me busy.

Thank you, Gisela Cabalang, who is part of our family and helps our family in so many ways. You know our success is based on your work and your foundation for our lives. At least, I hope you know, now.

Thank you, Nitish Jain and S P Jain School of Global Management (SPJ Global). You not only give me time to write but encouragement to push the boundaries of the Future of Education, as well as context in which to try out ideas on unsuspecting MBAs. Thankfully, there are no casualties yet, and they've been pretty happy with the new things I do, as well as the wonderful innovations you constantly provide them with.

Thank you to the SPJ Global FoW/FoE Think Tank members who shared, laughed, brainstormed, proposed, critiqued, and debated. You truly are an inspiration.

- Dr. Tal Ben-Shahar, Founder, Potentialife | Teacher of Harvard's Most Popular Course
- Paul W. Bradley, Chairman and CEO, Caprica International | Member, B20 Task Force on the Future of Work and Education for the G20
- Sarah Brown, Global L&D Operations Manager, Google
- Virginia Cha, Global Agenda Council Member, World Economic Forum
- Dr. Asli Chamizo-Toksal, Board Advisor on AI, Innovation, and Sustainability
- Dr. Edy Greenblatt, President, Execu-Care | CEO, Restoration Vacation
- So-Young Kang, CEO, Gnowbe | Chairman, Awaken Group | Young Global Leader, World Economic Forum
- Brian Ling, Design Director, Design Sojourn
- Dr. Chris Marshall, VP-AI, Analytics, and Future of Work, IDC
- Manoj Menon, CEO, Twimbit
- Jin Kang Møller, Author, Speaker, Designer
- Puneet Pushkarna, Venture Capitalist, Solmark | Chairman, Innoveo and Servion Global Solutions
- Jack Sim, Serial Entrepreneur
- Ashwin Sinha, CDO, Macquarie Group

Thank you, Paul Bradley, for the hours we spent over coffee discussing the future of education and your work at the B20 Task Force on Future of Work, Skilling, and Mobility. Your ideas not only made a difference in this book but are making a difference in global policy.

Thank you, Dr. Nic Hamelin, for sharing your leading-edge research on neuro-leadership and decision-making success through scientifically trackable intuition. We need to develop human potential in these spheres, and your efforts are trailblazing.

Thank you, Charles Phua, for inviting me to contribute this book to your brilliant series. You're right – we need more pracademics in this world with leading-edge ideas and the ability to make them real through practical application. Thank you, Routledge Editor Clarissa Lim and Editorial Assistants Chelsea Low and Khadijah Ebrahim. You've been great to work with and make a difference in the world, bringing ideas to light. Without Charles, Clarissa, Chelsea, and Khadijah, the ideas in this book would remain an underdeveloped strategy report buried on a shelf.

Please forgive me if I've missed someone. A book grows from many more people than just one author typing away until the manuscript is due.

Finally, thank you, dear readers. I pray this book will inspire you with ideas, spur you to action with examples of what others are doing now, and provide some initial guidance for what you will create.

Create something good. Our future is in your hands.

About the Author

Awarded as one of Asia's Top-10 Women in IT, Dr. Meadows leads an Innovation and Entrepreneurship Center at S P Jain School of Global Management – a Forbes Top-20 International Business School – creating growth initiatives at the intersection of IT, business strategy, and design.

Her research, teaching, consulting, and coaching span Design Thinking, Leadership, Creativity, Entrepreneurship, Sustainability, and the Future of Work (FoW) and Education (FoE).

She co-founded a Future of Education think tank that contributed significantly to this book and co-founded and chairs a corporation working for tiger conservation, ecologically and socially sensitive economic growth (sustainability), and people programs.

Holding a Doctorate in Business Administration and IT from Harvard Business School, Dr. Meadows has over 25 years of experience in Asia, Europe, and North America as a consultant, coach, entrepreneur, eBusiness builder, innovation lab co-founder, and Accenture IT and Business Strategy consultant.

Introduction and How This Book Can Help You

> I went to a bookstore and asked the saleswoman, "Where can I find the self-help section?" She said if she told me, it would defeat the purpose.
>
> –George Carlin

This book is an odd conglomeration of ideas, examples, and recommendations for the future of education that I hope inspires you and enables you to pursue your own education and provide future-appropriate education for others. The book is not competing with the classics in pedagogy, learning styles, etc. Indeed, the Future of Education will be an odd conglomeration of designs, business models, and technologies, serving a broader and bigger audience than ever before.

I wrote it for learners (sometimes known as students, but not always), parents, educators, education leaders, employers, and education-industry investors. In this context, "educators" include those on the front-line delivering education and those who design and administer. I also wrote a small section for policymakers, who can make a real difference in the educational context. That said, my primary audience is the front-liners who design, deliver, and consume.

Who am I to be giving education advice? I've spent years crafting learning journeys – including those for my kids – that the average educator or parent wouldn't, since I am (or were) a:

- Designer of educational programs for a private higher-educational institution
- Corporate consultant
- Entrepreneur
- Start-up mentor
- Homeschooling mom

I focus mainly on tertiary business education, but most of the ideas are also relevant to company learning and development (L&D), other fields, and other levels of education. I even include a section on primary and secondary education, since I encountered so much difficulty as a homeschooler that I'd like other founders, funders, and designers to be aware and make something for others that I dearly wished we had. (FYI, the term homeschooler is often used for both teacher and student, so I'll use it for both.)

I also focus on learning for work and life, not learning as entertainment. There's certainly a wonderful role in our lives for learning just for the joy of it. However, most people who learn for fun have at their fingertips a wide variety of affordable options, with books, clubs, Wondrium, MasterClass, the BBC, and more. I'll focus on people who struggle and need new options.

I begin with a chapter that basically shouts "FIRE" to establish that these issues can wait no longer. I then turn to Disruption and Design Thinking to share with you the lenses, tools, and techniques you can use to take action. Learners and employers are already struggling with today's systems, and new technologies and business models are already available to help us stop struggling. The following chapters outline particular struggles and needs we can design from, learning models we can use as "Lego bricks" in our new solutions, and specific business models and technologies we can use, with examples of who's doing what today.

I couldn't write a book about education without including a rant about the 250 million kids around the world who don't have a school – including mine (before they went to university), for many of their primary and secondary years. I also have to add that a further 300 million kids leave school unable to read and write – a crisis most people aren't even aware of (UN, 2023). I learned so much as a homeschooler that I had to share, and much of what I discovered in tertiary education can also help primary and secondary – and *vice versa*.

No one wants to hear just ideas and theories, so I included a very high-level sample design for one program (a tech-venture launchpad), disruption examples from beyond education that education leaders can use, and launch and growth options for new educational ventures. The final chapter pulls everything together and offers the next steps you can take now.

Overall, this book is meant to be an enabler, for you to start designing your own or others' learning journeys, be they your corporate employees, students, customers of your upcoming educational technology (EdTech) start-up, your kids, or yourself.

I wrote a multimedia companion book to go with this one so people could get an introduction to the issues and options, then come here for more comprehensive information. You can also work the other way – reading this book and going to the multimedia work for:

- Videos (especially attractive to visual and auditory learners!)
- A place to write your thoughts and next steps in response to action prompts and reflective questions, so you can apply ideas to your own situation
- Community, since other "readers" of the multimedia "living book" will be doing the same and can post their ideas and next steps on the book's community board for feedback and to find potential collaborators

What is a "living book"? It's a wonderful device enabled by technology just as our educational future is enabled. There are three ways in which it's alive:

- The materials can be continuously updated (so the **materials "come alive" and grow**), with no need to buy a 2nd or 3rd edition
- The focus is on applying ideas to real life and embodying them in a new design, new product or service, new business, life decision, etc. (so the **ideas "come alive" in action**)
- The readers/consumers can form community and relationships (so the **community "comes alive" to help each other**)

Digital resources can be found at drcjmeadows.com/futureoflearning, including a link to the multimedia companion book at GnowbeLearn™ (learn.gnowbe.com). Photos are copyright-free images purchased from depositphotos.com and are included to make your reading more enjoyable. (Modern textbooks are, after all, now covered in images!)

Thank you for joining me in this quest for the future of education. Use what's in these pages to change your life, your kids' lives, your enterprise, or create a new enterprise. Not only will you be glad you did, but those you empower will be glad, too.

1 We're on Fire!

Intelligence is the ability to adapt to change.

–Stephen Hawking

We Adopt Fast and Adapt (Too) Slow

Education is on fire, and it's students who burn.

According to the Education Data Initiative (Hanson, 2023), in the US:

- **Student debt takes on average 20 years to pay off**. A study by New York Life a few years earlier (DeMatteo, 2020) reported 18.5 years – from age 26 to 45. Imagine not paying off your student loans until your 40s!
- **In some professions, it takes over 45 years to pay off** student loans (making me wonder what was the point in the first place)
- **Salary for an average medical school graduate is not enough to cover their student loan payments**
- **21% of student borrowers watch their loan principal increase** in the first five years. Only 45% see it decrease
- The US Department of Education proposes ten years as the "ideal" time to pay off student debt (Does anyone else find that depressing?)

DOI: 10.4324/9781003340713-1

And yet, this is the age of disruption. Technologies are being adopted at shocking rates, and it's getting faster (Duarte, 2023; McGrath, 2019):

Table 1.1 Technology Adoption Is Getting Faster

Time to Reach...	*Surprising Stat*
1 million users: Threads	1 hour
1 million users: ChatGPT	5 days
1 million users: Instagram	2.5 months
1 million users: Netflix	3.5 years
100 million users: ChatGPT	2 months
40% of population (US): Mobile Phones	10 years
40% of population (US): Land-Line Telephones	49 years

That said, disruption is not just technology ("tech") adoption. It causes crisis in organizations and happens when you shake up an industry or create a new one (Perry, 2017; Mochari, 2016; Garelli, 2016):

Table 1.2 Industries and Companies Are Being Disrupted on a Massive Scale

Disruption	*Surprising Stat*
Fortune 500 companies from 60 years ago no longer on the list (bankrupt, acquired, merged, dropped off the list, etc., replaced by Google, Amazon, and others)	90%
Standard and Poor's 500 (S&P 500) companies expected to leave the list in 10 years (same reasons)	50%
Lifespan of S&P 500 companies in 1958	61 years
Lifespan of S&P 500 companies now	<18 years
S&P 500 expected replacement 2016–2027	75%

Most new industrial leaders are powered by new technologies, new business models, and virtualization, i.e. using as their core business foundation virtual assets like data, intellectual property, customer relationships, and systems, instead of physical assets. One of the world's biggest hospitality companies, for example, owns no real estate (Airbnb). One of the world's top transportation companies owns no cars (Uber). The world's largest bookstore owns no books (Amazon).

Although it all sounds very new, we're also returning to the old – but better. Family, friends, and community used to host each other in their homes and give each other rides. With technologies that enable community and trust among strangers, we now do that again via Airbnb and Uber. We used to get book recommendations from family, friends, and published writers, but now we can see reviews by people we've never met or heard of and use their recommendations to decide whether or not to buy a book.

What does this all mean for education? My big question isn't just how to do something new but rather how to fuse the best of what we had with the best of what can be. In the agrarian age, people learned to be farmers by apprenticing with more experienced farmers, listening, trying things out, and being individually coached. Blacksmiths, healthcare workers, apothecaries, and others did the same. In the industrial age, we embraced the assembly line and large organizations, which coincidentally required skilled people to be mass-produced just like the products they assembled. Schools grew into education factories.

In the knowledge age, we needed higher-order skills, so just like computer-enabled offices hungry for more workers, schools embraced computers and higher-order skills. Unfortunately, offices and schools still operated like factories.

With the advent of the creative age and its continuous, rapid (and often radical) change, virtual work, the growing gig economy, networked organizations, and work marketplaces, work environments are beginning to operate fundamentally differently – and so must schools.

In fact, not only can we recapture the personalized and practice-based education of the agrarian age and early industrial-age apprenticeships, but, like the new technological communities we now enjoy, our reach, variety, and access to learning will all explode – and the economics will change. Similar to technology-based communities, there will be dangers (fraud, identity theft and contracting, cyberbullying, hyper-structuring, etc.). However, as we innovate, we have always found ways to create new capabilities and capture benefits, while fighting dangers and drawbacks as they arise.

The most revolutionary technology today to enable the radical transformation of education is Generative AI (GenAI), e.g. ChatGPT. It strikes at the core of educational methods but is not, itself, a Socratic teacher or a system. As shown above, technology is being **adopted** quickly, and we now have a more difficult challenge: to **adapt** quickly and take advantage of the opportunities it and other technologies enable.

Disruptive education leaders and their investors are already building new organizations and developing or offering new services with currently available and currently emerging technologies and business models. They have a head start, and when they gather data from their forays into the market, they quickly clarify, pivot, adjust, and deepen their relationships with their customers and their grip on the market.

With some creative exploration into global offerings and technologies, students and parents are already cobbling together individual learning journeys to fit their particular needs (including at the university level), and this will become easier as enterprises follow their lead and launch for the struggling masses what the disruptive few are already doing.

Whether you're designing a new offering for others or yourself, don't start with your favorite, shiny tech toy. Begin with what people and organizations want from education and the skills and attributes they need for the future. Begin with some sympathy for the on-fire student loan figures above and their impact on people's lives.

If we radically redesign what is provided and how, incorporate new business models, and enable it with new technology, education should become far more effective, far cheaper, and achieve greater synergy among stakeholders – the ones that today are, in general, not satisfied (at best) and struggling (at worst).

Human-Tech Synergy and Future of Work: It's Already Here and Growing

Should we just pop new technology into old operations? Obviously, no. Not only will we have to learn in new ways, but we'll need to learn new things for a radically new world of work:

> Recent Accenture research suggests 44% of working hours across industries can be impacted by artificial intelligence i.e., Large Language Models (LLMs). … The research across 22 job categories also found that LLMs will impact every category, ranging from 14% of a workday at the low end to 76% at the high end. … Ultimately, every role in an enterprise has the potential to be reinvented, once today's jobs are decomposed into tasks that can be automated or assisted and reimagined for a new future of human + machine work.
>
> –B20 (2023, p. 22)

Try explaining to your great-grandparents your new job as an AI ethicist. You'll learn very quickly that you're living the future now. The Future of Work (FoW) that we're developing requires skilling and reskilling for future jobs (or tasks), some of which don't even exist today (like your job as AI ethicist, which was offered at Microsoft in 2018 and described as an ethical code for AI systems by Isaac Asimov in 1942).

We see growth in the silver and inclusive economy, growth of "informal economy" and diverse forms of work, including gig work, agency, self-employment, job sharing, part-time, apprenticeship, fellowship, volunteer work, and crowd work. Worker mobility is increasingly needed (both physical and virtual), and lifelong learning has become a mantra for small- and medium-sized enterprises (SMEs) and entrepreneurs, as well as big businesses, to stay abreast of technological changes that enable new possibilities. We'll transform jobs, create new ones, and address problems we haven't had the resources to solve until now:

> As highlighted by a recent OECD report, the future of work presents exciting opportunities with the potential for automation to transform 14% of current jobs and create new ones. Additionally, with 32% of jobs

> having the potential for partial automation, it is a chance for workers to develop new skills and take on new roles, driving substantial progress and growth.
>
> –B20 (2023, Executive Summary)

Will the classic professions change? Doctors, lawyers, CPAs, architects, and other professions may change the most, due to the quantity of think-work that can be taken over (or augmented) by artificial intelligence (AI) and Gen AI. One of my colleagues visited an architectural practice with an 11-year-old girl, and after asking a number of questions to the architectural team on their current project, the girl used her AI tools to produce architectural designs, four furniture/interior décor samples, and estimated costing in just four hours. The professional team had planned a few months for that work.

What's left for humans to do, and what skills will we need?

> Advances in AI, robotics, and automation will reduce the need for manual, repetitive, and basic cognitive skills, while increasing the demand for technological, social, emotional, and higher cognitive abilities. Similarly, the green transition will push for new products to be developed. This will require new skills, but changing product cycles will also create unexpected new skills demands, as manufacturers may focus more on prolonging the product life cycle by investing in repair networks, or efficient use of resources by smarter planning.
>
> –B20 (2023, Executive Summary)

Part of the journey will be to improve the dialogue and collaboration between employers, learners, education providers, and policymakers who can support career transition skilling, education financing, national skills projections, and more. However, dialogue (multilogue, actually) cannot take the place of action. We need to co-create, which is also a key skill for this new age.

Our "learn-earn-return" industrial-age career model is now lifelong learning, earning, and returning. Almost 65% of millennials won't accept a job from a company without strong CSR practices that "return" to society. Fully 80% of CEOs believe that skilling is their biggest business challenge, and learning has become employees' second most important driver of workplace happiness (right after the actual work they do) (Bersin, 2019).

So, industrial-age schools that only trained people pre-employment will have to adjust to a new world of meaningful work and lifelong learning.

We Only Have 5 Years to Burn – Not 15

Do I actually believe we only have five years to change, or did I include that just because some expert told me (Bradley, 2023)? Another expert (Kang,

2023) shared some time ago that the digital transformation of existing organizations takes about five years.

Given that some educators have already started the transformation process (more than mere technology adoption) – some named in the following pages – yes, I do believe we'll see new organizations and offerings transforming our learning lives in five years or less. My belief is reinforced by FoW and AI research that point to necessary and widespread reskilling needed within the next five years and ongoing reskilling needed every five to ten years.

Why haven't we created the future already? Simple: we're better at adopting than adapting. But look at lead users. Some of us have already started.

You can, too.

2 Disruption and Design Thinking

Two Keys to Unlocking Tomorrow's Education

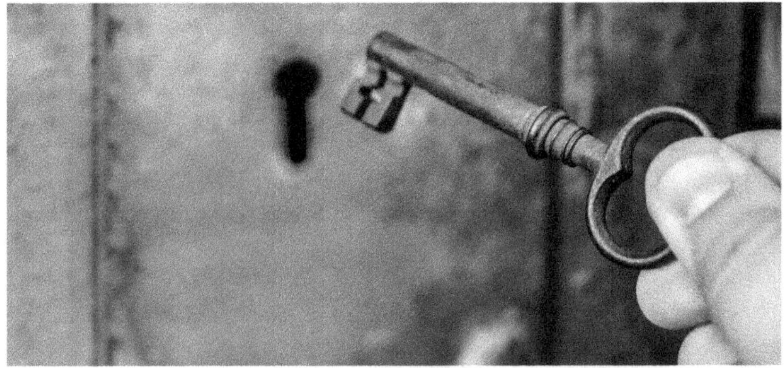

Imagination is the only key to the future. Without it none exists – with it all things are possible.

—Ida Tarbell

Education is something of value. People not only work hard to learn but often put themselves into debt for it – sometimes leading to decades-long financial crisis. When base-of-pyramid communities are asked what they want from aid organizations, the first two answers are usually healthcare and education – and not always in that order.

Like a safety deposit box that requires two keys, we need two keys to unlock the future of education – disruption and Design Thinking. One tells you when the conditions are right for change and how it can happen, the other helps you craft the change. First, I'll share with you what they're about and how they might be useful. Then I'll guide you through the rest of this book using these lenses and language.

DOI: 10.4324/9781003340713-2

First, How to Get a Law Degree in Three Years Instead of Eight

When my son announced he wanted to become a lawyer, I was a very happy mom and didn't experience the succeeding panic most parents have when they stop and think about it – panic over the cost. I knew we'd find a creative way to handle it.

David was 16 years old when he shared his interest with me. He'd just finished his IGCSEs (International General Certificate of Secondary Education, roughly equivalent to British O-levels). For students heading to university ("uni"), this would generally be followed by A-levels (General Certificate of Education Advanced Levels) for two years. (Or, if you're going to Hogwarts, OWL O-levels in the fifth year, followed by NEWTs in the seventh year, which I assume are A-levels.) Then, since he wanted to practice in the US, he'd need four years of undergraduate education, followed by two years of law school. So, the path would be two years of A-levels, four for a bachelor's degree, and two for a master's degree.

Eight years.

I spoke with an international lawyer friend, and she shared that she knew lawyers in the UK who were surprisingly young. They shared with her that a law degree in the UK is generally a three-year undergraduate degree, followed by an exam similar to the bar, to become a practicing lawyer. So, if David went to a physical uni in the UK for his education, he'd only have to do two years of A-levels and three for a bachelor's degree.

Five years.

Then my older son, who had finished A-levels, was headed to uni. After looking at global options, we decided on Open University (OU) in the UK, which was online and would allow him to live with family in our home in Singapore, continuing to see his friends and girlfriend (and occasionally mom, dad, and siblings, when necessary).

Big surprise when filling out the registration materials: no A-levels required. With over two million alumni, that couldn't be an oversight. So why do physical and most online uni's require them? For certain fields, e.g. math, medicine, and the sciences, a bachelor's degree will build on the A-level materials. For most (including my kids' fields of business, law, and psychology), it's not necessary. The bachelor's program will cover all you need to know for the degree. OU was created to help people get their degrees, not stand in the way.

Wow.

So, cancel the plans for A-levels and associated fees just to age two years and start careers later (losing two years of income). Let's all go to uni! (All four of my kids, that is). David's journey could be simply three years for a bachelor's degree, followed by the bar exam in the US or the Solicitors Qualifying Examination (SQE) in the UK. (Yes, my friend said the UK and US systems are similar enough that it's no problem to study one and switch to the other. International lawyers do that and more all the time.)

Three years.

When I gave him a choice between the three journeys, what do you think he chose?

Three years, of course (a relief to me, too, since I'd have to support him during all those school years).

Bonus: OU produces more law graduates than any other institution in the UK. My son is in good company – and a lot of it.

What does this mean for you? Simple: have you explored systems beyond the one you grew up with? I'm American, so I knew nothing of all this, beginning with what on earth is an O-level. There are different systems of education that might greatly benefit you, your kids, and/or your educational customers. And where that's "the system", people often assume that's the only system, too.

Call to action: when you find ways around your system or a better way through another one, use it and share your epiphany with others who'll benefit, too. (You might even write a book about it.)

What else does it mean? Not all the innovations you'll create or use are technological in nature. Although OU is online and thus offers locational flexibility, it has been a leader in "distance education" for over 50 years – since before the Internet. The real innovation for us was the lack of A-levels requirements (advanced level exams generally taken at 17 or 18), as well as using the UK legal education system (law undergraduate) instead of the US.

What will happen after the degree when it's time to take the bar exam (US) or the SQE (UK)? Law graduates can (1) study on their own, (2) take an online or in-person course, or (3) hire a tutor. When I did my CPA and CMA exams, I studied on my own and did just fine. Again, each learner has their own style and needs, and now there are loads of options.

What Is Disruption, How Does It Work, and How Can We Use It in Education?

Disruption happens when you shake up an industry or create a new one. Uber, for example, shook up the taxi industry and also created a new one – ride-sharing. Table 2.1 discusses ten things you need to know (and might have assumed incorrectly).

Table 2.1 What You Need to Know about Disruption

No.	*Disruption Insight*	*So What? For Learners*	*So What? For Start-ups*	*So What? For Incumbents*
1	**Disruption and "business as usual" don't mix.** Running today's business and creating tomorrow's is about as easy as changing the tires on your car while you're driving it.	Seek innovative programs that fit your needs cheaper and better, but realize the bugs may not be fully worked out yet – like new software. If you want bug-free, you may have to go for a traditional (and expensive) solution. FYI, When I say expensive, I'm including not only tuition but also having to relocate to a physical campus, maybe giving up your job in the process.	Consider Co-CEOs. Someone can run the business while the creative disruptor (and team) creates. Ralph Lauren used this two-leader strategy when Ralph grew tired of running the business instead of designing, and the business suffered. MenuLog used this strategy and wound up with a USD 750 million IPO (initial public stock offering). Co-CEOs are becoming more popular partly for this reason. Avoiding burnout is another good reason.	Ditto.
2	**Disruption starts at the bottom** of the market, with consumers who can't afford what's on offer (non-customers) or are overpaying for what they actually need (overserved customers).	Think deeply about what it is you really need and want out of your education and consider new, non-standard offerings. Consider "bottom of the market" offerings if you just need a degree and skills to get a job. Big brand names (Harvard, Stanford, Yale, etc.) often make more impact on a *curriculum vitae* (CV) at graduate school and can make almost as much impact via executive education (in much less time).	Start at the bottom of the market with overserved customers and non-customers. Give them exactly what they want without the extras and in radical, new ways. Once you've got a profitable minimum viable product (MVP), focus on scale.	Look out for competition at the bottom of the market – the consumers you may not focus on or care much about. If you want to keep them, set up a disruptive innovation team to serve them in radical new ways. (More on that below in number 9.) Consider open innovation, collaborating with actual start-ups instead of relying only on in-house innovation.

3	Disruptors "eat their way up". Incumbents give way to disruptors when they both "move up the value-added chain" focusing on higher-profit-margin goods, services, and customers.	Consider growth when choosing an education provider. You might choose a growing program from an incumbent or, if it's exciting and exactly what you want, a non-traditional player.	When developing disruption theory, Clay Christensen's original question was, "Why do successful companies fail?". The shocking answer was, "because they did nothing 'wrong'". It's long been an accepted practice to focus on high-value portions of business, but it can also mean an incumbent allows itself to progressively shrink itself out of existence. Use this to your advantage.	Instead of letting go of portions of the market, consider spinning off portions of your business to operate differently, keeping the whole company in a portfolio and maintaining a category brand.
4		Again, figure out exactly what you need and want and don't pay for unwanted extras you can avoid.	Don't try to compete at the top (unless it's a new market area), and don't be seduced by fancy.	Consider developing "inferior products" that are not scaled-down versions of what you already offer. (When was the last time your boss asked you to do that?) Understand your low-end users and give them exactly what they need – no more.

(Continued)

Table 2.1 (Continued)

No.	*Disruption Insight*	*So What? For Learners*	*So What? For Start-ups*	*So What? For Incumbents*
5	**You have to focus on the Job to Be Done (JTBD)**.	Spend some time on these questions before making choices: (1) "What am I really trying to do/accomplish?" and (2) "What do I really want?". Then consider 50 different ways to get that job (or those jobs) done. You may see yourself in the Design Thinking section below, which introduces different JTBDs for education.	Decide which JTBD you'll serve and give users exactly what they need for it. Design Thinking can help you discover what "the job" is and design for it. Remember: you have to be better just to launch and survive.	Again, decide which JTBD you'll serve and give users exactly what they need for it. Use Design Thinking to discover the JTBD and design the solution. Thankfully, brand recognition and customer loyalty may give you some leeway while you're developing, launching, and expanding, but don't forget the start-ups that may be snapping at your heels.
6	**Top and bottom need to talk**. Top executives have the power to launch innovation programs and offerings, but front-line workers are the ones who continually sense needs and problems that become new products, services, and solutions.	Share your JTBD with education representatives. They can either help you find an already-designed solution, or you may have to design something yourself since you probably can't wait for a company to listen to you and offer your solution. Consider starting or joining a start-up, in which you'd both understand the need and have the power to craft solutions.	Make sure your leadership and customer service folks communicate. Some start-up leaders (or, indeed, all the staff) spend some time serving customers on the front-line to help them listen, learn, and stay focused on users.	Ditto, plus it may be a good idea to create infrastructure to capture insights from the front line. This can include physical (e.g. the old suggestion box, which some companies find provides millions of dollars of value), online equivalents, and social (e.g. incentives, sharing what happened with ideas, an ombudsman, town halls, and innovation workshops).

7	**Technology is not enough.** It's not inherently disruptive, and you can't just "throw tech at it".	When considering programs, ask yourself if this is just the same old experience that's been stuck onto the internet or if there really is a newer, better design (e.g. more experiential learning, apprenticeships, "live" projects, enhancing your learning/discovery skills so you can continue life-long, etc.).	Don't spend all your time on the technology. First design your solution to be radically different from today's offerings, then support that with tech.	Instead of just replicating what you do with tech, redesign what you offer (or what you don't, yet) and make organizational changes to support that (including good change management). Set aside some resources (including people) to "mess with" new methods and tech that enables new methods you won't know until you "mess with it".
8	**It's all about RPPs** – resources, processes, and profit formula.	Sorry – this one's not for you.	Figure out not only your offering and tech, but also the resources, processes, and profit model you'll need. Too many start-ups focus solely on the offering, not on developing the organization/business. In fact, you're lucky to launch now. When "dot-coms" first started, they had two business models – (1) inherent business value and (2) advertising. Now there are over 20.	When IBM extended its offerings from mainframes to minis, personal computers (PCs), start-up services, design services, and more, each offering required different RPPs. They succeeded because they didn't tie up new, inherently different businesses with RPPs from old. New businesses were run as separate businesses (under the category brand). A mainframe sales team, for example, has a long sales cycle with expensive people diagnosing client needs and designing unique solutions. You can't do that for mini and PC sales.

(Continued)

Table 2.1 (Continued)

No.	*Disruption Insight*	*So What? For Learners*	*So What? For Start-ups*	*So What? For Incumbents*
9	**Know who'll win before you start.** With a disruptive innovation, the start-up (or spinoff) will win, but only if what it offers is ten times better than today's solutions. With a sustaining innovation (helping the incumbent make money in the way they're already designed to), the incumbent will win, even if it's only a 10% improvement.	If you want to sign on for a truly disruptive offering (one that shakes up an industry or creates a new one), you may want to sign on with a start-up, spinoff, or relatively new player. If you want a standard, old offering, you should probably choose a well-established player and offering.	Ask yourself if you're truly disruptive and ten times better than today's solutions (so people will try you out). Are you shaking up an industry or creating a new one for customers who are over-served or who can't be served at all? When Airbnb launched (actually, the final of eight launches), they succeeded by offering rooms around major conferences with booked-up hotels. If people wanted to go to the conferences, Airbnb was the only choice. Likewise, Uber became popular around concerts and sports events with a shortage of taxis. People had to take Uber or face real difficulties getting home. So, launch for customers who have to use your service or just get by on their own. That said, if the service could be done by an incumbent with their existing RPPs, you may have to join them or find something else to do.	If you see disruption coming (like everyone else in the education industry), consider setting up a disruptive innovation center as MetLife did with LumenLab. Ideas could come from MetLife or LumenLab, and the lab would develop solutions. Sustaining solutions that make money in a way that aligns with existing organizational design to were introduced back into the parent business. Disruptive solutions were spun off like start-ups. In general, disruptions have to be kept away from a core business because the core business will kill them (since they'll attack the core business and ruin executives' performance metrics and bonuses).

10	**Prioritize profits BEFORE scale, use "emergent strategy", and specialize (no longer one-stop-shop).**	Sorry – this one's also not for you.	Don't let your venture capitalists pressure you into launching before you have a stable, profitable offering UNLESS they're happy to lose a lot of money (many are) and it's a race to capture a market (e.g. Amazon being funded for years until they were profitable, because a marketplace platform has to be dominant to win). Don't try to use deliberate strategy like a corporation. That was my job before entrepreneurship, and I couldn't do it. Start-up strategy evolves from a series of experiments with different offerings, where you gather data and learn. As an industry matures and especially as it's disrupted, pursue a modular, specialist strategy.	Don't let your senior leaders pressure you into launching before you have a stable, profitable offering. It's a great way to meet your deadlines and lose many millions of dollars (as quite a few companies have learned). Although you're well-versed with deliberate strategy, your new initiatives may really be experiments with no existing data. Adopt an "emergent strategy" approach, in which you test, gather data, analyze, adjust strategy, rinse, and repeat. This will cause huge headaches for the sponsor who has to defend the initiative and blow past deadlines, but it could save you millions and promote later success. Rethink your current one-stop-shop strategy and identify what to "unpack", modularize, and specialize. As industries mature and especially when they're disrupted, dis-integrated specialists do well.

Given that many of education's customers are over-paying for what they really need or can't afford it at all, is the education industry ripe for disruption?

I think you know the answer.

Is adding videos to existing courses disruptive? No, not if it's just embellishing an existing offering using the existing RPPs (resources, processes, and profit model).

Will everyone race to do things differently because new tech has opened up new possibilities?

No. They need a "burning platform".

What is that? I learned the hard way.

When I was getting my doctorate, I got very excited about the new global ICT (information and communications technology) infrastructure worldwide. I could envision people working seamlessly in teams across the world and companies getting the best talent at the best prices, breaking through local shortages. Following the globalization of manufacturing, we could finally globalize services. Virtual teams would proliferate and change not only local manpower constraints but also our way of working, living, and urban infrastructures.

I researched extreme projects to learn more about how to manage such work – complex, high-coordination services – in short, software production by emerging economy consultants for developed-economy companies.

When people heard what I was studying, they said, "you're researching what? Where? That'll never take off".

It was Indian outsourcing.

It did "take off" (the industry earned nearly USD 9 billion this year), but the practices and lessons learned didn't transfer to other work.

Why?

I did my research in the early-to-mid 1990s, and even when Skype and Zoom were founded (2003 and 2011, respectively) – offering mass infrastructure for virtual work – people and organizations had no reason to change.

But eventually, they did.

COVID struck, and suddenly, people had to work in virtual teams on a mass scale. COVID was the "burning platform" that prompted people to leap into something new.

I won't delve into post-COVID virtual work issues, but I will point out that over-served and not-served customers already have a burning platform (in any industry, not just education). If you launch and grow your offerings for them, you can later extend to others once your offering is established. Witness how many people now choose to take Uber or Grab when they could take a traditional taxi instead.

So, the education industry is ripe for change, but how can we discover those Jobs to Be Done and design offerings for them?

That's where Design Thinking comes in.

What Is Design Thinking, Why Would We Do It, and How Can We Use It in Education?

Design Thinking is a human-centered approach to innovation that draws from the designer's toolkit to integrate the needs of people, the possibilities of technology, and the requirements for business success.

– Tim Brown, Chairman, IDEO

The quote above is the best definition I've found. Design Thinking (DT) is a great way to address human-centered challenges where you don't have a solution and you don't fully understand the problem, either.

Research shows it to be highly effective for product and service development, as well as crafting customer and employee experiences – and student experiences and services. In fact, design-oriented companies have been shown to outperform competitors and industry averages on a number of performance measurements, with up to (Sheppard et al., 2018; Jaruzelski et al. 2014):

- Two times industry-average growth (McKinsey Design Index)
- Three times operating income growth (strategy&/PWC)
- Two times shareholder returns (McKinsey Design Index)
- Two times ROA (return on assets) (strategy&/PWC)

The list goes on. Forbes called data science and DT "the new power couple" (Meléndez, 2022) because data science can point you to where problems are, but you need an approach like DT to understand why the problems happen and what to do about it.

I could rattle on for days about DT. In fact, I often do, when I run MBA and corporate executive education workshops and sprints. For now, though, you'll probably benefit most from the same "Ten things you need to know" format as above, so please refer to Table 2.2 for the essentials.

If you'd like to learn more about DT, I can of course recommend my book, multimedia book, articles, and webpage with more links and resources, at drcjmeadows.com/designthinking. For now, we'll just use these key concepts as we look at education and what we all might create for the future of education.

Table 2.2 What You Need to Do about Disruption

No.	*DT Insight*	*So What?* *For Learners*	*So What?* *For Start-ups*	*So What?* *For Incumbents*
1	**DT can create huge value when you use it for human-centered problems that are complex, where you don't really understand the problem yet and have little or no data**. It's not for pure-tech optimization, simple challenges, and fully known problems with no "discovery" needed.	You can use DT in your personal life (not just for business) to understand your needs better and come up with creative options you may not have considered. I recall someone who did that to help them get married and discovered they were pursuing marriage for the wrong reasons. There were so many less-dramatic options for fulfilling their needs – a life-changing exercise.	Start-ups that have leaders or board members with design expertise actually succeed better and attract more funding, because they are more solid on the needs they're serving, design offerings more creatively, and reduce cost and risk by prototyping and experimenting earlier, quicker, and more often. That said, when the marketplace is highly uncertain and completely new (or just beginning to take shape), and user desires are more malleable, you may want a "grand designer" approach like early days Apple and WeChat. You'll want a diverse team for DT and should plan on three to six months for a project.	There's plenty of research showing that if you have an innovation dollar to spend on an appropriate challenge (see columns at left), DT is the most productive (or at minimum, a very productive) approach. Give it a try if you aren't already.

2	**Start with desirability**, then move onto technological feasibility and business viability.	Again, delve into what you really want out of your education before you make big decisions.	It's so easy to fall in love with tech and its possibilities (see section above on my love of ICT and virtual teams). However, organizations and offerings that lead with the tech – instead of what people need and want – often fall into "shiny tech syndrome" and fail.	Ditto
3	**Work on the right problem/ challenge.**	Deconstruct your challenge (e.g. with a "challenge map" – you can Google it to learn more), so you can understand (1) why you want it (is it strategically important and gets you other things you want?) and (2) what's stopping you (maybe you need to fix that first?). My daughter took this approach and realized getting up on time wasn't the problem to work on – going to bed was.	Do a challenge map (see column at left) and also "right-size" your challenge so it's neither too big (inspiring but ultimately unworkable) nor too small (unlikely to lead to radical, impactful innovation). Remember, you have to offer something ten times better than the incumbent to win as a disruptor.	It's shocking to see smart people create brilliant solutions for the wrong problems. But they so often do. Teams sometimes work on problems just because they were told to. Unfortunately, if the boss didn't take the time to set up the right problem, the solution will fail. Do a challenge map and right-size the challenge before you begin (see columns at left).

(Continued)

Table 2.2 (Continued)

No.	*DT Insight*	*So What? For Learners*	*So What? For Start-ups*	*So What? For Incumbents*
4	**Observe and interact**.	Although designers generally observe and interact with other people, you can do this on yourself, too. Is there a difference between what you do, say, think, and feel? You may have great educational intentions, but what you do and feel generally trumps thinking and talking. Observe yourself as if you were solving a problem for someone else. Have a conversation with yourself, too, asking probing questions. Make sure you observe and talk with people in the job/career you'll have after your education, too. Shadow some for a day if possible.	Make sure you're designing from real observations and questions answered by real people, not out of your head and from the tech-based opportunities. You might think Meta (formerly Facebook) introduced something so new that there were no needs before social media. Wrong. Facebook tapped into social needs that already existed and gave people a new way to fulfill them. Disruption theory teaches us that needs are the basis of a stable and growing business. How we fulfill those needs will change. Witness Netflix, which originally served users via the postal service. Read the column at right, too.	Ditto the columns at left, and get out of your office to do your best, most productive work. Observe and ask questions of extremes – folks who hate or can't use your offerings (to discover what's wrong) and those who completely love your offerings (for good ideas for the rest). Pursue analogies outside the education industry (or different age groups, etc.) for good ideas you can bring back to your situation and use, like the emergency room team who got great healthcare ideas from a Formula 1 pit crew.

5	**Understand deeply**.	Map what you do, say, think, and feel about education and what it'll do for you (i.e. make a persona or empathy map). Write down some of your new insights about yourself and what you really need and want from your education.	Splay your qualitative data all over the wall and use informed intuition to identify the motivations, thoughts, and feelings behind what people do. You may uncover deeper insights from one observee or from connecting two or more. These insights are what you design from. It helps to have a diverse team with different perspectives and co-creation, co-thinking skills. Try finishing the sentence, "Sometimes, people …" in multiple ways.	Ditto.
6	**Envision a radically better future.**	Once you've identified what you really want and what's standing in your way, generate as many ideas as you can for fulfilling your needs – both "normal" and wild. Don't worry initially that they're too wild. They'll spur more workable ideas, or you may bring them down a notch and make them workable. Aim for more than 10–20 ideas, since the first ones will be boring. You get to the creative gold afterwards.	Ditto at left, plus remember not to judge ideas when you're generating. Let every idea out and announce it to the team (usually a team that does DT) so it can spark ideas in other team members. When you have 35–50 ideas on a wall or flipchart, identify the ones you feel the most energy around and have a conversation about them until you've converged on one. Take that one forward.	Ditto at left, plus remember that corporate teams tend to judge ideas when they're generating, so they often don't share the really creative stuff because "we won't get budget" or "leadership won't support it" or "we wish we could, but it'll be too hard" or another thousand reasons. If you get radical envisioning, you're more likely to come up with something high-value and impactful – and ways to make it happen – rather than incremental tweaks that are a waste of design time.

(Continued)

Table 2.2 (Continued)

No.	*DT Insight*	*So What? For Learners*	*So What? For Start-ups*	*So What? For Incumbents*
7	**Solve the real problem**.	Look at your vision and in more detail, solve the "real" problem(s). Draw it, write it out, talk it out, make a journey map (again, you can Google that to learn more), list what you'll gain, what you'll spend (money, time, and other resources), what you need to do, and any risks and how to mitigate.	Ditto at left, and be sure you take the customer's perspective (you're your own business), when you outline the gain, cost (money, time, and other resources), to-do's, journey, risks, and mitigation. Consider whether your solution is really ten times better than what people are doing now to solve this problem or fulfill this need. If it's not, go back and get more radical.	Ditto, plus consider whether this fits into your current business – your resources, processes, profit model, other offerings, brand, etc. If it does, it's OK to create a 10% improvement (of course, more would be better). You could make it an offering or use it to enhance a current offering. If it doesn't fit your RPPs, you'll want to spin it off. If you keep it part of your category brand, it won't have to be ten times better than your customers' alternatives, since your brand will attract people. However, the bigger the improvement the better, since you'll have to compete with start-ups who are aiming for a ten times improvement.

8	**Prototype and experiment**.	If you're considering a degree program, you could begin with certifications, courses, and work experience that'll then get you credit in the program(s) you're considering – from that institution or others. Many schools now give credit for "life experience". It's possible to use the early part of your degree to try out different fields or topics, but instead of only classroom exploration, consider working in different fields, either paid (beginner-level) or as a volunteer, before full-time study or concurrently. You'll get a feel not only for the work and lifestyle, but you'll be able to observe more and ask more questions than on a "shadow-day".	Although this is the last step, it takes half of DT project time and is done iteratively until you're not learning much more and have a pretty solid offering. Make sure you don't just do focus groups and a survey. Get people in a room with cardboard boxes, roleplay, storyboards, and drawings of customer experience, services, and computer/phone screens. See how they actually behave with the prototypes, and gamify their options. Make your prototypes "low fidelity" – cheap and quick. Understand before you interact with real people what you want to learn from them. Generate new understanding, not just yes, I'd buy this service, or no.	Ditto, and resist the temptation to devote big budgets and make end-stage prototypes early on. Make early, sloppy stuff out of paper, cardboard, etc. and invite people in who could be customers (or are disgruntled ones), to learn more about what you've made and what they want.

(Continued)

Table 2.2 (Continued)

No.	*DT Insight*	*So What? For Learners*	*So What? For Start-ups*	*So What? For Incumbents*
9	**Add an agile loop to the end to work on technological feasibility and business viability**, on the way to launch.	If you've decided to sail around the world while getting an online degree and write a book about your experiences (for example), investigate others' experiences doing so, the technology, and the finances – both spending and earnings along the way from a variety of sources. Influencers get sponsorships and go on some amazing journeys (e.g. Kraig Adams, the hiker). Make some small runs before the big journey. You could even propose to chronicle your student journey for a school's school marketing, in exchange for scholarship support (why can't schools be influencer sponsors, like Sony or Land's End?).	At the end of a DT project, you've established the desirability of your offering, but you don't have a complete offering yet. Spend some time getting the tech and business model right, then do a soft launch (hotels do this for a reason), revise, repeat as needed, and do the hard launch – then scale.	Ditto.

10	**Just do it!**	Not only can DT help you in this education-design circumstance, but the skills of innovation, framing unstructured situations, discovery, understanding deeply, envisioning the future, creative problem-solving, critical thinking, co-creation, and experimentation are part of tomorrow's skillset in the age of generative AI. DT is conceptually easy but hard to do well until you've done it for a while, just like riding a bicycle. Practice now and use these skills over your whole lifetime.	Not only can DT help you craft your offering, but becoming a design-oriented company should improve your business performance along a number of dimensions, as mentioned above. How can you lose, designing what people need and want and having employees with the skills at left?	Ditto, and start with some small projects and quick wins while you build support for the DT approach. Not only can DT help you craft or re-craft your offerings, but the skills should spill over into all areas of operations. Remember to publicize yourself as a design-oriented, innovative company, to attract customers, employees, and shareholders.

How Might We Use Disruption and Design Thinking Together?

In sum, disruption's JTBD and DT's "needs and wants" are the same. Disruption shows us, from an industry and customer perspective, when the time is right for change, how it generally happens, and who will probably win.

Given a situation that needs change, DT helps change-makers understand what's needed and design (and refine) new solutions.

In short, disruption theory shows us the time to act is now, and DT can help you do it.

Recommendations for Students, Educators, and Investors

Students

Beyond the specific recommendations in the tables above, the big message for you is to stop yourself from simply doing what's been done before and paying a very high price for it. Take the time to do a little Design Thinking on yourself and your own situation and take charge of your educational design. Even if you use a program designed by a school, you'll need to supplement it with work, internship, volunteering, certifications, and more. There are some great certifications on EdX and Coursera, and when you list them on LinkedIn, begin the description with the school brand (e.g. Harvard, Stanford, MIT, etc.).

If you still need to learn a bit more about yourself, below are some of my favorite resources. I highly recommend HBDI (Hermann Brain Dominance Indicator) and other psychometric tests. My executive education partner and I ran HBDI sessions for Panasonic-Matsushita executives, which meant I had to take the test, too. I sorely wished I had done it 20 years earlier so I wouldn't have had to wander around different fields and jobs discovering what was not a good fit for me, on the way to discovering what was – a very expensive exercise, indeed!

- HBDI (Hermann Brain Dominance Indicator)
- MBTI (Myers-Briggs, and a free version is available, called 16 Types)
- DISC
- Ikigai
- eParachute.com
- CliftonStrengths, from Gallup
- Basadur Innovation Profile

Apparently, about 70% of success is not a direct result of your intelligence quotient(IQ), so I also recommend learning more about emotional intelligence (EQ), positive psychology, and an online visit to ResilienceOasis.com. You can find links and more resources (e.g. favorite articles) at drcjmeadows.com/coach.

Educators

You're in a disruptive situation, and either you and your organization will change now, or you'll be left behind. If you're not familiar with how your offering is not serving people well, use Design Thinking to find out.

As a front-line educator, you can't change your organization's business model overnight, but you can propose programs with new models – to be run independently, else the larger organization will kill them. If your organization won't change and is headed for disaster, it's probably time for you to look for another one that will change. You could also consider joining or founding an EdTech start-up. You'll need to experiment with the technologies in this book (at least some) so you'll be able to show you're curious, skilled, and seeking to build the future.

As an education leader, consider launching spinoff programs and projects as innovation experiments. At a minimum, you'll gain brand value for showing you're innovative. At a maximum, you'll have profitable spinoffs that lead to the future of your business.

Will the spinoffs cannibalize your existing business? Perhaps – or perhaps not. You may simply attract a new customer base with different needs. If your spinoffs do cannibalize your business, wouldn't you rather they do it than someone else?

Whatever approach you take, remember to begin with needs. Understand people deeply and choose one or a few needs/wants to pursue. Don't try to boil the ocean and all its schools (no fish pun intended). Then envision and design a far better future that fulfills those needs in a radically better way. And don't forget the prototyping and experimentation. Don't scale before you have a profitable Minimum Viable Product (service, actually) – unless, of course, you want to burn through investor money and take over a global market.

Investors

Along with creating disruption theory and the Innosight consulting firm, Clay Christensen founded an investment fund focused on disruptive enterprises. Last I checked, it earned 35% above other funds in its asset class. Education is ripe for disruption, and there are returns to be made.

If you're a venture capitalist (VC), you're probably fine burning through money before an offering is profitable, if you're grabbing a global market in which there will only be one winner. My VC friends continually shock me with how much money they're happy to lose trying to produce one unicorn out of a portfolio of possibilities.

If you're a more traditional investor, however, be wary of pressuring new-offering leaders to scale before they're solid and profitable. It's a great way to lose a lot of money.

No matter what kind of investor you are, you should know that start-ups with designers in the leadership team or on the board succeed better, faster, and attract more funding. If your investee leadership does not include design expertise, consider pushing for it to be included with one or more design leaders and enough staff to support a design-led approach to service and business development.

3 Start with Needs

Who Is Education's "Customer", and What Do They Want?

Why Start with Needs?

Until you understand your customers – deeply and genuinely – you cannot truly serve them.

–Rasheed Ukunlaru

"Shiny-tech syndrome" is rampant among technology start-ups. I should know. I'm a technophile, an entrepreneur, and have been part of the start-up scene since the term eCommerce was coined (sadly, without Bitcoins for the clever nomenclator).

What is "shiny-tech syndrome"?

When technologists get excited about a new tool and think everyone automatically wants to rush forward and use it, that's "shiny tech syndrome". Too many start-ups have failed by leading with tech, and too many corporates have failed by leading with their own business needs.

People care about their own needs (yes, even the altruistic among us), and if you want to succeed, you have to start with that.

The best illustration I know is the milkshake story, which I first heard from Scott Anthony, of Innosight fame plus his work with Clay Christensen, the originator of disruption theory.

DOI: 10.4324/9781003340713-3

Basically, a fast-food chain wanted to win in the "milkshake market", so a consultant went to an outlet and observed for 18 hours what was going on. (At least he didn't go hungry). There were two spikes in sales: 7 a.m.–8 a.m. and after school.

At around 7:30 a.m., the consultant asked a middle-aged man who was dressed in a suit, wearing a wedding ring, and buying a milkshake why he was buying a milkshake. The man replied that he had a one to one-and-a-half-hour commute to the office and needed to both fill his tummy until lunch and stay awake and alert during the drive. What else had he tried? Coffee that left him hungry a half-hour later, a banana that was hard to peel and eat while driving (and left him hungry an hour later), and a bagel that was hard to spread cream cheese on while driving.

In the afternoon, he observed a father and son apparently getting an after-school, after-soccer treat. The father was middle-aged, dressed in a suit, and wore a wedding ring. The man kept looking at his watch, asking his son if he was finished. The poor boy was drinking as fast as he could without getting brain-freeze. Clearly, what should have been a happy treat became just another stressful event.

When I take Design Thinking workshop participants through this example, they inevitably design for the morning commuter a thick, coffee-flavored shake with skinny milk (or almond milk, soy milk, etc.), and a thin straw – maybe with little crunchy surprises to slurp up, too. For the afternoon crowd, they design a thin, chocolate-flavored shake with whole milk (and whipped cream and sprinkles, of course), and a thick straw.

Are these two products milkshakes? Yes, in the sense that a Rolls Royce and a Volkswagen Beetle are both cars, and both Harvard and your local community college are schools. These products and services, however, are successful not because they're independently well-designed. They're well-designed for particular needs and wants. The commuter shake and the happy-family shake are very different products.

There's an important lesson for strategy, too: is there a "milkshake market"? What is your market? Your competitors are not those in your industry as *you* define it. They're your customer's alternatives, from the *customer's* perspective.

There's an important lesson for design and marketing as well: although we love to use easily measured demographics (think: married, middle-aged businessman), it's the psychographics that really matter. What's your customer's JTBD? Their needs and wants? Designers create a "persona" (often with a short, meaningful name) from which they design that includes what an archetype customer does, says, thinks, feels, and ultimately – needs and wants.

What does this have to do with education?

Everything.

If you don't understand what your customers are trying to get done and what they do, say, think, feel, need, and want, your offering may not fulfill them. Once another offering comes along that fits them better, they're gone.

First, Changing Needs for Skilling, Reskilling/Upskilling, and Silver Skilling

Before delving into various needs and how to serve people better, we should understand why education is the way it is, as well as older models that may be newly available with digital tools.

In the agricultural age and the early industrial revolution, people learned through individually taught apprenticeships that combined work and learning. The upper echelon of society went to schools that used the Socratic method to develop individuals' thinking. All very personalized.

Gutenberg came up with the printing press, which enabled mass-produced books that enabled mass-produced people (students/workers) for the industrial age. Books were coupled with factory-style learning methods, and large organizations hired the schools' products – people. We continued to use those methods in the knowledge age to mass-produce workers for growing bureaucracies still designed in the industrial-age style.

Now, in the creative age, we're returning to non-factory-line types of work and embracing open and networked organizations. The "gig economy" continues to grow and represents 36% of the US workforce. People are rediscovering apprenticeships, the Socratic method, and personalized education, but this time with new tools like AI teachers and digital resources.

Education is still needed for workers entering the workforce, and two groups are increasingly joining them:

1. **Current employees** needing reskilling and upskilling to keep up with digital transformation and grow their careers, and
2. The **"silver generation"**, which faces both discrimination and ever-increasing life expectancy. Many of them need not only digital skills but also entrepreneurship skills, to keep earning in an unfriendly marketplace

So, employer needs have changed, and learner needs have changed. Let's examine them in detail.

What Do Customers Need from Education? What Are They Buying?

Employers

> just under 30 percent of companies believe they have the digital talent they require, and a Wall Street Journal survey showed that 89 percent of executives struggle to find candidates with the right mix of soft skills – things like teamwork, communication, and adaptability. … A stunning number of students learn little in college.
>
> –Horn and Moesta (2019)

> You have to invest in every one of [your employees] because if they don't learn new skills, they lose all their value within three to four years. … We're looking at recertifying the skills of every worker every three to five years for the rest of their life. You don't even have a choice. You have to invest in upgrading.
>
> –Paul Bradley, speech at the B20/G20 CII Partnership Summit

Employers of course need to recruit employees (or gig workers) and ensure they have the skills to do their jobs well. Far from routine and successful, the quote above suggests it isn't going well, and the problem is becoming more acute. Reskilling and upskilling are also a growing mandate, and employers have to ensure their employees have new skills or face the more costly (and, given the above, difficult) problem of replacing them.

There's another need – new ideas, network, and help for the business – commonly available to large corporations via executive education with thought-leader experts. SMEs, unfortunately, are often locked out of that market due to high fees.

How can educators help? By extending some of what they already do or launching new offerings to serve these needs. As an employer, are you asking educators for these services? As an educator, are you offering them? You may need to take a moment and consider three needs employers commonly struggle with and start demanding new offerings.

According to the World Bank (n.d.), 90% of businesses are SMEs, and they provide over 50% of the world's employment, as well as up to 40% of GDP in emerging economies. They will likely grow in importance as advanced technologies continue to democratize production. Although they're often locked out of high-end executive education, they need access, and new technologies and business models can be used to make services like the above more affordable and scalable.

Table 3.1 Employer Needs

Persona	*Employer JTBD/Need/Want*	*Opportunity to Extend Today's Services*
RecruitingCo.	"Help me find/develop job candidates".	Superior recruitment and placement with, for example, psychometric and skills testing pre- (or post-) admission, powered by AI, including neuro-testing. (Most employers don't have a neuro-lab.) Attribute and skills tracking could be updated throughout an alumni's career, enhancing (sometimes introducing!) such tracking by employers.
CorporateSchool.	"Help me get out of the business of running a corporate school".	Outsourcing non-strategic parts of corporate education; paid access to individual degree-program classes; access to faculty-expert mentors and/or coaches; 360-degree feedback (bosses, colleagues, supervisees) before and after educational programs to assess the business impact (i.e. track educational productivity like any other activity).
ClientCo.	"Help me get fresh solutions to business problems" (basically, this need is for non-traditional consulting or open innovation).	Blended education and consulting ("edusulting"), leveraging workshop time for decision-making and innovation; extended coaching and mentorship to implement what's generated or decided in workshops; apprenticeships or other mixed learning and working, with trackable business and learning outcomes; paid access to faculty mentors and/or executive coaches; projects and "sprints" engaging employees and students together.

Students

Globally, there are both free and low-cost university programs not everyone may be aware of. University of the People (UoP), for example, is the first tuition-free, accredited, online, American university. Their mission is to provide access to higher education worldwide, promoting both peace and economic growth globally. Shai Reshef's TED talk outlines how it was put together with materials donated from top institutions (e.g. Harvard and Cambridge), staffed by an extensive network of volunteers, and supported by an impressive array of partners (e.g. the Gates Foundation).

At the time of the TED talk, a four-year bachelor's degree cost $4,000 – with financing available. Similar to Coursera and EdX, learners pay for testing and issuance of degrees, not for their learning.

Why do people still incur huge debt? Some are probably not aware of alternatives, and some are afraid the alternatives won't be accepted when job hunting. According to UoP's website, 92% of degree graduates are employed, including at organizations like Amazon, Apple, Deloitte, IBM, the World Bank, and more.

Whatever the reason, school choice and offerings design need to be rooted in learner needs, such as in Table 3.2 (expanded from Horn & Moesta, 2019; Christensen et al., 2010).

JTBDs by students who don't "hire" higher education, and new JTBDs during technological and economic upheaval (of which we'll see more), are outlined in Table 3.3, based on informal interviews with students, non-students, workshop attendees, conferences with educational professionals, etc.

Some students don't want to miss out on changes in the marketplace, so don't take "time out" to go to formal school programs. This is fairly common in technology fields and in fast-growing markets like China.

One solution is (again) to offer market-based learning. Harvard's MBA program includes a summer work requirement in an established company or start-up (which can be launched by the student). Indonesia's Minister of Education – himself founder of a start-up now worth over $12 billion – announced that if a student wants to go to work for a start-up for a year and it's approved by the dean, he or she will receive a full year of university credit.

Designs like this show us that education can serve needs well, stay current, and be more affordable.

Is There Still a Need for Curated Programs, and Is an "Open Degree" Worthwhile?

Yes, people still need curated programs. Although self-directed learners can design terrific programs for themselves, it takes a great deal of time and learning to do so. An expert can design far more quickly – and cheaply, per learner – a program that'll yield well-rounded expertise in a field, function, or industry. Design by experts is still worthwhile from a time, cost, and content perspective.

Table 3.2 Learner Needs

Persona	*JTBD/Need/Want*	*Implications for Schools*	*Opportunity to Extend Today's Services*
TopSchool.	"Help me get into my best school".	Big-name schools (and "prep schools") are already here and will probably stay. That said, schools with less brand recognition increasingly partner with big-brand companies. NASA-JPL programs, for example, are in high demand, and certifications are offered by companies like IBM (sorry – no degree programs yet).	Top schools hesitate to offer online, blended, and part-time programs. My husband, who has degrees from Cambridge, U. Chicago, and Harvard, continually struggles to find his next degree fix (yes, he's a learning junkie). He won't compromise on quality or brand and won't give up his day job. If you're a small brand, consider partnering with the very top corporate brand for something truly innovative that will attract learners.
The Dutiful.	"Help me do what's expected of me" (subtext: "my parents say I have to get a degree, but I don't know who I am or what I want").	Provide an "expected" degree, beginning with helping the student understand him/herself and crafting a personalized developmental experience.	Offer psychometric and skills testing and coaching pre- (or post-) admission, powered by AI, including neuro-testing. Personalize the educational journey so the "duty" is fulfilled AND the learner grows in ways s/he wants.
The Escapee.	"Help me get away" (subtext: "I want to get away from my job/life").	Once this learner "gets away", s/he may not actually know what to do – a very different problem from knowing what *not* to do. As above, start the program with diagnosis (helping the learner understand him/herself), then help him/her choose life direction(s) and pursue.	Help the learner "get away" (physically or topically) and begin with diagnosis and personalization (see above).

(Continued)

Table 3.2 (Continued)

Persona	*JTBD/Need/Want*	*Implications for Schools*	*Opportunity to Extend Today's Services*
The Ambitious	"Help me step it up" (subtext: "I want a better job/life and need qualifications or something to achieve it").	Provide the necessary qualifications/resources/opportunities as clearly and efficiently as possible. If possible, offer modular, flexible programs whereby learners can skip what they already know ("life credit") and focus on what they need to "step up".	Enhance your offerings with fast and/or flexible delivery (including online/offline), professional networking the student can't achieve alone, and superior job placement, assisted by psychometric diagnostics and skill tracking.
LearnerGrower	"Help me extend myself" (subtext: my life is good, and I want to grow into something I like or towards my next step").	Help people grow themselves and/or their skills without disrupting their lives.	This need is currently filled by physical and online programs, as well as edutainment (e.g. Masterclass.com and Wondrium). Offerings should be low-cost, with fast and flexible delivery. Consider offering personalized coaching and networking opportunities (including lifestyle networking).

Table 3.3 Learner Personas, JTBDs, and Opportunities

Persona	*"Student" JTBD*	*Opportunity to Extend Today's Services*
The Dropout.	"Help me finish something" (subtext: "I don't have the discipline to do it without being pushed/structured, and I hate doing it alone").	Online programs for qualifications abound, but 40–80% of students don't complete them. Enhance these with AI and personal coaching and tracking. Consider blending with in-person experiences, making a hybrid program, since face-to-face programs have a 5X completion ratio. Consider centralized content and online delivery with franchised physical experiences with facilitators you've certified (which is, coincidentally, another source of revenue).
The Disrupted.	"Help me explain a 'CV gap', gain skills to re-launch my career after a gap, or gain experience no one will give me without experience – and get a job". (Note: current employers sometimes won't authorize new-experience opportunities, and it's certainly a problem when searching for the next employer. "Gaps" include systemic job loss during economic upheaval, taking time to take care of family, etc. "Silver generation" workers are included here for digital skilling and general upskilling).	Provide actual experience doing what the person wants to be hired to do. Mentoring will be key, and many employers don't want to (or can't) provide it. Again, offer superior job placement services with psychometric diagnostics and skills tracking mentioned above.
The Entrepreneur.	"Help me learn how to run a business, because I have an idea, existing business, or generally want to be an entrepreneur". (Note: "Silver generation" users are also included here so they can survive in an unfriendly marketplace).	Offer mixed learning and working, with business outcome(s). Start-up incubators and accelerators can extend their offerings to these customers or partner with educational institutions.

That said, when my son wanted a dual degree in marketing and Christian theology, I was impressed by the creatively diverse interests. I also began to envision new jobs in marketing ethics, faith marketing, and more. Of course, we didn't find that some expert had already designed one (yes, I actually looked), but I did discover a bachelor's degree called an "Open Degree" from Open University. It allows a student to choose from over 250 classes across 16 subject areas and create a personalized bachelor's degree.

In my research into high-value innovators (Meadows, 2020), I found cross-disciplinary learning and work to be a precursor of radical, high-value innovation. Bill Gates is known for his "think weeks" in which he learns from multiple disciplines in order to address vitally important problems facing humanity today. One of my colleagues who (with the rest of his founding team) launched his start-up's $850 million initial public offering (IPO) of stock recalled how he'd take classes at university in a wide range of subjects but never took a degree.

Did my son do the Open Degree? Sadly, no. We thought it would be easier to get a job with a more common degree in a single field. He chose marketing and continues theology and church leadership on his own. In the context of lifelong learning, he may later earn a theology degree and many more certifications – and perhaps combine his fields in new and innovative ways.

Do I believe an Open Degree will become more accepted and popular? Yes, I do. Cross-disciplinary have existed for some time, and as we partner more closely with our technologies (requiring creative, deeply thinking humans); as jobs become more personalized; and as humans address more difficult problems best solved with creativity and multidisciplinary approaches, I believe such personalized education (with compelling stories to explain the design) will provide an "edge" over more standard, commoditized job seekers.

Perhaps I'll get one, myself.

Can We Mass-Customize?

Happily, this is the age of mass customization. Even Nike now lets us design our own sneakers. In education, we have the technological capabilities to diagnose individuals' attributes and skills, assess market opportunities with systems like Epitome, modularize learning units, combine them in flexible ways, and provide AI tools to coach and assist learning. All we need to do is employ the technology and share expert-crafted designs alongside hyper-personalization options.

What's standing in our way?

My best guess is (1) brand concerns, (2) business model, and (3) accreditation. Schools guard their brands religiously and are notoriously concerned whether new offerings will dilute standards and the brand. Educational programs undergo a lengthy design process, and it takes time to reap the benefits. Schools hesitate to throw anything out (thus shortening the "run time") or introduce something that might cannibalize today's offerings. Finally, accreditors review every design, and offering a design that's basically no design may be a challenge. That said, Open University got the Open Degree accredited. Schools have to have enough faith in a design/offering (and learners who'll hopefully sign up for it) to undergo the significant time and effort required to gain approval.

Ultimately, maybe it's just faith in the new that holds us back.

Recommendations for Students, Educators, and Investors

Students

Does one of the personas above describe you? More than one? Look for offerings that particularly fit your needs and supplement what you find with your own designs, where your chosen provider isn't following all the above recommendations.

Before taking a standard offering to get a standard job when you start, consider customizing. In the industrial age, we designed jobs (and programs), then molded people to go in them. In the creative age, we'll assess what individuals have to offer and manage tasks, not jobs – basically molding jobs to people. You may be better off getting something standard now and customizing yourself and your career as you go. Or, if you have particular passions and desires and don't fit "the system", know that you can choose to customize yourself and your qualifications now.

An acquaintance of mine failed his O-levels and A-levels. He didn't do well in school because he was such a talkative, inquisitive child – and because the school had repeated staff changes that disrupted everyone's learning. Without O-levels, he couldn't get his A-levels. Without A-levels, he couldn't get a bachelor's degree (if only he'd known about Open University and others that don't require them). He took a job and became a top salesman (talkative and inquisitive were good things, after all) but couldn't be promoted without a bachelor's degree. So, he launched 16 successful businesses and eight social enterprises (not all at once). He "retired" at 40 to launch the social enterprises and later earned two master's degrees (without a bachelor's).

If more flexible programs were offered to this clearly talented person, would he have taken them? Would they have helped or held him back from his ultimate success?

I don't know. All I do know, from writing about a 13-year-old dropout who became a Michelin Star chef and other successful innovators is this: education has been structured in a way that doesn't fit everyone (for more stories, see Meadows, 2020). I also learned that their roads to success were harder than they might have been because they were working "outside" the only system available at the time.

It's time for more personalized systems, work, and learning.

Educators

Are you struggling to serve one or more of the personas above? Are your offerings really designed for particular personas and their needs, or are they just general-service offerings you hope will catch enough customers in your net?

It might be time to hire some designers to do some qualitative research (research is for businesspeople, too, not just academics!) on your current customers and non-customers. Find out what needs you're not serving well (or at all) and what needs you may want to serve. Take a design-thinking approach and learn deeply about people's needs and constraints before you design and offer. Open your mind to new business models and technologies and the potential of a category brand, with different sub-brands and offerings included.

Investors

Have your education investees identified which of the above personas and needs they're serving? How rigorous have they been in researching needs and addressable markets? Do they have designers deeply understanding users, designing from insight, and prototyping with users, or are they led by their own fascination with technology, their own business model, or tradition? If you're considering whom to invest in, consider that design-led start-ups succeed better.

Push for design-led offerings and a design-led business if you haven't already, with designers in the leadership team, a formal design unit and practices, and a "critical mass" of design awareness across the organization.

4 What to Learn and How, for This New Age

What to Learn: A New Model

How many lessons does it take for a human to learn to drive? About 20. How many lessons for AI to do so? About 10 million. There's a lot of power in AI, but a lot of power in humans, too.

–Dr. Chris Marshall, VP – Data Analytics and AI, IDC Asia Pacific

If Google, ChatGPT, robots, and other technologies can learn, know, and think (depending on how you define these activities), what do we need humans for? The work we do and the lives we'll live will determine the learning we need, so that question gets to the heart of both Future of Work and Future of Education.

DOI: 10.4324/9781003340713-4

The short answer is that we'll need people who can:

- **Ask** great questions of their AI pals (and in general)
- **Evaluate** and **question** the results AI gives them
- **Synergize** well with tech (and humans!), to produce the best of both worlds
- **Investigate**, **learn** from, and **make decisions** in situations that are ill-defined or where there is little data AI can work with
- **Act** in the physical world to make decided things real

> Judge a man by his questions rather than by his answers.
>
> –Voltaire

Further, we have scientific evidence for intuition and its connection to decision-making success. The data reveals that our intuitive capabilities can not only be tracked but also developed (Hamelin & Bonelli, 2022) – something our advanced technologies don't (yet) have.

Beyond intuition, emotional intelligence is a highly sought-after job skill:

> Financial expertise and operational experience will only take executives so far. More than ever, companies want senior leaders with strong social skills and emotional intelligence.
>
> –HBS Working Knowledge (Fitzgerald, 2021)

According to LinkedIn Learning research on business talent (much of which can be extended to other fields; Brodnitz, 2024), **communication ranked #1 among all in-demand skills**, and people skills will be central to career growth. 90% of global executives agree that soft/human skills are more important than ever, and over 50% of LinkedIn's 1 billion members across 200 countries and territories hold jobs that will be disrupted or augmented by AI.

What's the full list of the top ten skills? In order, it's:

- Communication
- Customer service
- Leadership
- Project management
- Management
- Analytics
- Teamwork
- Sales
- Problem solving
- Research

They all sound very human to me.

The **skill that grew most in importance: adaptability**. In fact, the speed of learning both knowledge and skills may itself become a prized, trackable attribute.

As a professor and education designer for a global business school, I researched what sort of graduates we should be developing for the future. The attributes and skills I gleaned from predictions by the World Economic Forum and other research for tomorrow's businesspeople were numerous and varied.

To make some sense of it all, I put each one on a slip of paper and laid them all out on my desk. I moved them around, grouped them, and removed duplicates. The framework that emerged (see graphic) grouped the attributes and skills into elements of being, thinking, and doing. The LinkedIn skills mentioned above are embedded in the framework, either directly or as outcomes of the more foundational skills in the framework.

The attributes and skills in the graphic include:

- Doing
  - Running Today's Business
    - Established technology skills
    - Org/admin/managerial skills (incl. goal setting and planning)
    - Functional skills
  - Creating Tomorrow's Business
    - Emerging technology skills
    - Entrepreneurial/intrapreneurial
    - Emerging topics (social impact, environment, wellbeing, security, privacy)
- Thinking
  - Logical
    - Analytical/critical
    - Judgement/decision-oriented
    - Strategic
    - (Eco)systems thinking
  - Creative
    - Creative problem ID/framer/solver
    - Info: find, analyze, use
    - Integrative
    - Flexible/agile
- Being
  - Intra-Personal
    - Open/curious
    - Positive/confident/self-esteemed
    - Courageous/considered risk-taker
    - Energetic/passionate
    - Independent

    - Self-aware
    - Self-developer/learner
    - Self-disciplined/directed/ motivated/managed
    - Passion for excellence/quality
    - Comfort with ambiguity/uncertainty
    - Ethics/integrity/character
    - Persistent/committed/diligent
    - Resilient/resourceful
- Inter-Personal
    - Questioning (also intra-personal)
    - Communicator and negotiator (listen/understand/ respond; clear)
    - Composed (respond constructively to emotional situations, high pressure, and conflict)
    - Comfortable in unstructured environments
    - Connective/collaborative/co-creative and team-skilled
    - Empathy (perspective, emotion, compassion; serves and develops others)
    - Leader
    - Crisis manager

Basically, we need people who can do today's work and create tomorrow's, hence the two types of doing in the graphic. We also need both creative and logical thinkers, hence the two types of thinking. Perhaps most importantly, as the foundation on which our thinking and doing are built are two elements of being – intrapersonal and interpersonal.

It surprised me that most of what I was discovering was not doing or thinking – the focus of most of today's education. **Most of what we would look for in future graduates would be elements of being, suggesting we need more character-based, transformative education**. That actually makes sense to me now, because if much of today's doing and thinking will be handled by AI and other tools, we'll need to focus on what our tools can't do and can't think, which will stem from our human "be-ing".

> The cyclone derives its power from a calm center. So does a person.
>
> –Norman Vincent Peale

When I showed the FutureSkills framework to one of my FoW/FoE think-tank members, she shared that she wished her education – particularly her Ivy-league MBA – had focused more on her character:

> Three years into my new venture, I found all of my character flaws embedded in my organization. Now I wish I'd dealt with them before launching an enterprise.
>
> –Tech Founder

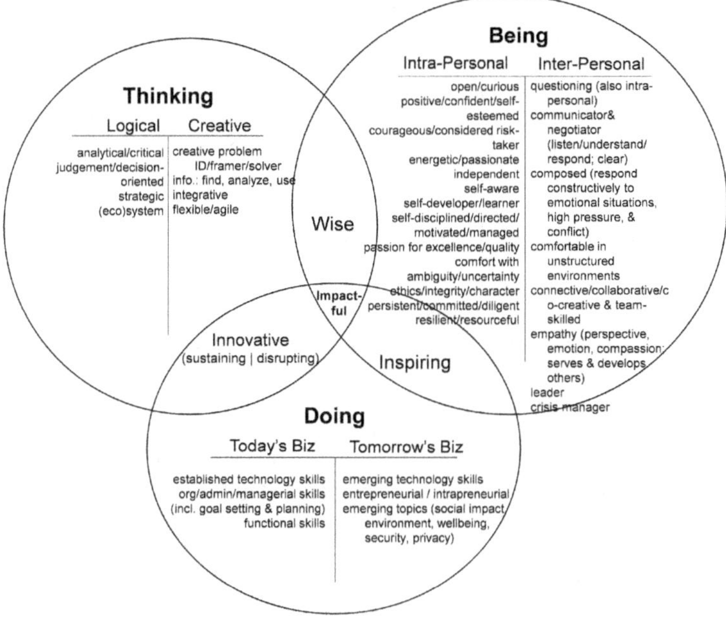

When I really looked at the FutureSkills framework bubbles, I also started thinking about the intersections. When we combine doing and thinking, optimally, we end up with innovation. When we combine doing and being, we become inspiring. When we combine our being and thinking, we can become wise and share our wisdom in significant ways. When we become innovative, inspiring, and wise leaders, we can make a real impact in the world. Our best leaders aspire to this, and as people, that's when we become our best selves.

How might education designers use such a framework?

The learning objectives for "courses" and "units" (in today's accreditation terms) could be based on these six categories: inter-personal and intra-personal skills, logical and creative thinking, and skills to run today's and create tomorrow's businesses. In fact, a similar framework of being-thinking-doing was independently developed for leadership education at Harvard Business School (but not with these particular categories and skills). These six categories could themselves be six different certifications, and the individual attributes and skills within them could be micro-certifications.

Increasingly, schools are parsing their degree programs as collections of certificates that stack into personalized degree and diploma programs – Lego-style. Learners welcome the flexibility and the sharable recognition of their new learnings and skills along the way, especially those who both work and learn at the same time, a practice I predict will continue to grow.

Whether beginning a program full- or part-time, participants should begin with the intra- and inter-personal "being" attributes/skills, since that is foundational to setting and achieving both life goals and educational goals. Helping participants with these "issues of being" can also be a key differentiator, since most schools – even in the Ivy-league – still either skip this step or don't do it fully and well.

If We Can Augment Ourselves with Technology, Do We Need to Learn?

> Human augmentation technologies may shape what we will need to learn. Google Glass is already launching technologies that allow you to see how other people feel so you can learn to understand other people's emotions better. [Yes, the Enterprise Edition devices still work.] Skype is now able to translate languages in real time, so you don't need to learn a new language. Cerego is an app that tailors your learning to memory science so you can retain information better. Adult learning will be greatly shaped by human augmentation technologies. Technology advancements are expanding both the modes of learning as well as increasing what can be learned. With a potential exponential increase in global ambiguity and complexity, this may push adults to go back to the basics of morality, character, and life topics while encouraging a mindset of lifelong learning.
>
> AwakenFutures (part of Awaken Group, 2023, p. 10)

Now that technology auto-translates in real time, do we still need to learn languages (for example)?

Yes, because language isn't just about words and grammar – it's also how you use the words and grammar. Ideally, a digital translator will work out the words and grammar for you, but you need to figure out what you want to communicate and how – content-wise, culturally, and interpersonally.

I (and others!) foresee a future in which every person has an augment, e.g. a digital twin. Not only will we perform our tasks with digital help, but we'll educate our twins and learn (and remember) from them, too. We'll benefit from their learnings from the broader world, and they'll benefit from ours.

Further, one of the things I learned from studying creativity is that we create with the ideas and skills already in our heads, i.e. our unique mental workshops. Then when we have an initial creation, we tap into our social and other networks to collect other ideas, skills, and people to develop it.

In short, we still need stuff in our heads from which to create, as well as skills for targeted collecting and collaborating.

Augments don't do that.

But they can help.

How Much Reskilling/Upskilling Do We Need, and Whose Responsibility Is It?

> According to the World Economic Forum, 50% of all employees worldwide will need reskilling by 2025 due to adopting modern technology. By 2027, over two-thirds of skills considered important in today's job requirements will change. A third of the essential skills in 2025 will consist of technological competencies not yet regarded as crucial to today's job requirements. While some employers do anticipate the need for reskilling, just 37% of HR professionals stated that upskilling and reskilling the current workforce were likely to be top priorities for their organizations in 2023.
>
> B20 (2023, p. 42)

The B20 quote above clearly indicates that major reskilling is needed, but employers are not geared up to provide it. They will need to do something, and fast, given that replacing an employee now costs 50–200% of an employee's annual salary (McFeely & Wigert, 2019) – even if you can find new people with the new skills you need while every other employer is looking for them.

Companies used to provide skilling, reskilling, and upskilling, then reaped the benefit via lifetime employment (still a common practice in some nations, although declining). Now, despite ever-increasing employee turnover, many find they have to provide education because they can't find candidates with the skills they need – and to avoid cost and business disruption from employee churn. Governments like Singapore, which pays up to 90% of skills-training costs, are also taking the lead in reskilling and upskilling.

That said, ultimately, learners have to be in charge of their own development. Yes, avail yourself of company training and government funding, but especially with the proliferation of affordable online learning and self-development, the learner leads.

How to Learn: New and Old Learning Models for This New Age

Once you deeply understand for whom you're designing a learning journey (including yourself), you'll want to have a variety of models and approaches in the back of your mind. Don't forget to explore old models that can be revitalized and scaled with new technology.

The old can become new again. After all, in the last century, people used to give each other rides in their cars. We stopped when communities became less cohesive, and stranger-danger entered everyone's minds. Now we do it again with Uber and Grab, with technology-tracking for safety.

You may not have thought about the models below, but each one has a key lesson to inform your design decisions.

Montessori: Student-Desire-Based Learning

Maria Montessori, a pediatric physician and psychiatrist working in the late 19th century, observed that children confined in mental asylums needed more stimulation. She began to work with children once thought unteachable and achieved surprising results.

She developed (and then scientifically validated) a method of education focusing on learners' natural curiosity, independence, activity-based learning driven by their own interests, and real-world skills. Her approach is based on providing a supportive, well-prepared learning environment and does not include tests, grades, and other conventional measures of achievement.

Her method fits well with Design Thinking. Designers know that providing external incentives often fails. You'll run out of money (or other resources) trying to pay people to do what you want them to do – and they'll still find a way to do what they want. The key to success is usually finding out what people want and care about and helping them achieve **that** in a new way.

Ironically, teaching Design Thinking in an educational setting with the traditional trappings of accreditation – tests, grades, grade curve, etc. – I stumbled upon students that truly did not want to learn what I had to teach. I didn't even know why they were unhappy with the experience until I used the new technology I'd already instituted in the course in a new way.

With the Gnowbe platform (discussed in the technology section below), on which I had placed their multimedia textbook, I discovered a shocking number of them had not been through any of the material and had not even registered on the platform. Then they complained they weren't learning much.

Imagine! When you went to uni, did the school know if you bought a textbook – and whether you opened it – and how much time you took going through it – and how many exercises you did – and more?

Now you can.

Given the setting in which I taught, my smart colleague said, "Just treat it like a virtual absence and apply our policies to that".

I did, but I also wondered to what degree I should be pushing people to learn who really don't want to. Should I be monitoring progress or outcomes? At what age does a learner take charge of his or her own learning?

Montessori is a popular method for preschool. Surely uni students are old enough? In a Harvard Business Online course I took, each video had to run completely to get to the next action (yes, Gnowbe can do that too), but should I design that way or encourage more exploration in learners (and the ability to skip if they already know something), since they will need to manage themselves in a world to explore and learn from?

I suggested we make the course optional when we do our regular re-design. That said, it is key to the FutureSkills framework above. Learners who trust their designers will go along with expert design. However, in this case, I suspect the learners were pushed into a program they didn't choose and didn't pay for.

Lesson: Learner interest comes first. As best you can, design an environment and programs/activities that tap into what people want to learn and inspire trust in the expert designer to learn what they don't yet know they need. You may be able to start uninterested learners with everyone's favorite topic: themselves. If you begin with self-discovery and have a flexible enough structure to engage them actively, you should be able to back into what experts declare are key skills, instead of leading with those skills and getting to application later (see Lumiar, below).

Gamification: Fun, Rewarded Learning

Most people agree that gamification can make learning more engaging, but do gamified formats with instant feedback, points, and progression through game levels actually get better results? According to KPMG research with a client's optional gamified leadership training focusing on the company's offerings (Does Gamified Training Get Results?, 2023), fees grew 25+%, client numbers grew 16%, new-client opportunities increased 25%, and the more people used the game, the more they improved their job performance. Offices with more willing learners grew fees 16% more than other offices, and offices with more leader gaming grew fees and new clients 19% and 7% better than other offices (respectively).

Do the results show that gamification always enhances learning over non-gamified formats? No. But it does show that learning can make a measurable difference to work performance, and gamification can make learning attractive and engaging. After all, people voluntarily set aside their "real work" to use the game and chose how much to engage with the game.

Lesson: Try gamifying your education, and track the results you're looking for. At a minimum, you'll provide a more fun, engaging, positive experience. Optimally, you'll get people addicted to learning and have better results.

Lumiar: Project-Based and "Expert-Led" Learning

Declared one of the most innovative schools in the world by UNESCO, Lumar is grounded (like Montessori) in learner interests, independence, and activity-based learning. Each student (age 0–14) has a personalized curriculum in the form of a "Digital Mosaic". Learning is tracked on the mosaic as they progress through cross-disciplinary project-based learning.

Multiple ages are included in "learning cycles" that focus on specific developmental needs for each age group, and the traditional teacher role is broken into tutors (who facilitate learning and will stay with each child for two to three years) and masters (of particular content, generally professionals), thus engaging the traditional master/apprentice approach and tutoring/facilitation.

Students (at least the older ones) set their own rules and govern. Their regulations are strikingly similar to other schools but decided and "owned" by the students. Projects are proposed by students, and not only do tutors and masters evaluate learning, but students constantly self-evaluate. Learning is displayed via audio/videos, debates, reports, photographs, presentations, podcasts, posters, and other means.

The use of experts to teach learners is not confined to Lumiar. S P Jain School of Global Management (SPJ Global), for example, welcomes a significant number of senior practitioners to their faculty, combining the rigor of doctoral-degreed faculty with real-world-expert faculty. To facilitate their participation, courses are not given over a four- or six-month term, but rather, in two-week sprints (most practitioners can get away from the office for a "teaching vacation"). Long-term assimilation and integration of learning are ensured with full-term projects and assessments.

Lesson: Learning journeys can be customized and tracked with technology, and each learner's custom curriculum can be envisioned as a mosaic. Learners can take charge of their own journey with project proposals, student governance, and self-evaluation, and learnings achieved by projects can be recorded on a mosaic of skills. Instead of desired skills driving activities, desired activities can drive skills.

Teachers don't have to be experts in everything if you break up the role into experts and facilitators. In fact, we should harness the talents of the experts all around us to share their knowledge, skills, and wisdom, especially with high student-teacher ratios resulting (sometimes) in lost learners with little help but Kahn Academy and YouTube. Our designs, formats, and schedules need to help experts get involved, e.g. via sprints or part-time projects.

ACE: Student-Led, Coached Learning

Facilitation and coaching are also a key feature of the ACE School of Tomorrow®. Their curriculum and approach have been around for over 40 years in 145 countries for millions of students. Teacher conferences are attended by 20,000 participants per year. Although controversial due to the Christian fundamentalist material and uniqueness of the approach, its impact is undisputed.

The school is "flipped", i.e. using an individual-study approach. Teachers are called "supervisors" and do not lecture classes like the common, industrial-age school model. They come to students when asked and coach students through the material to find their own answers and develop their own understanding. The approach is especially useful now, in the age of IT and globalization (ubiquitous internet), when it's critical that students learn how to learn, how to find information, and how to reason through it themselves.

From age five, students plan their own daily goals, study the curriculum on their own (with coaching as needed), and mark their own quizzes and self-tests. The approach is highly individualized (along with group activities, sports, arts, social time, etc.), and instead of the standard approach of fixed schedules with variable learning (graduating at a specified age whether the student has mastered the material or not), students have to learn the material to progress but can take as much (or little) time as they need – fixed learning with variable time.

The room is inverted, as well. Students sit facing the wall around the perimeter of the room, as opposed to traditional classrooms with theatre seating or group tables and students facing the teacher or each other. Further, the material and age are decoupled not just in general but also by subject. For example, a student can learn standard history materials for her age group, highly advanced math, and fundamental English. Leadership of self and of others is fostered, via group activities, projects, and taking special roles to help others (e.g. special-needs students, who are integrated with the cohort).

Lesson: Instead of being sage-on-the-stage, effective materials and self-testing can free up teachers to be more effective as coaches. Learners can plan, self-evaluate (with reasonable controls), and manage their own learning even as young as five years old. We can uncouple time and curriculum, focusing on mastery (including advanced, average, and foundational studies all at once), albeit with alerts if learners are moving so slowly that overall progress is unacceptable.

In fact, Sal Kahn shared that Kahn Academy data yielded a surprise: when learners slow down to master something difficult, they then sometimes become the fastest – and vice versa. In a traditional curriculum, learners who hit a rough patch may just fall behind or drop out. Flexible pedagogy and technology can help them stay in the game, moving fast, then slow, then fast again.

Stanford and Harvard Business Online: Learning Communities

> Who, what, where, when, why and how people teach and learn are rapidly becoming more democratized. Green School in Bali is pioneering transformative learning pedagogies that offer primary school students control of their own learning journeys. Xingwei College in Shanghai gives students the power to hire and fire their own teachers. Ecole 42 in Paris has no teachers, no textbooks, no MOOCs, and no tuition and yet it is more competitive to get into than Harvard.
>
> AwakenFutures (part of Awaken Group, 2023, p. 9)

Stanford created a terrific vision of the future of education, in which learners enter a community, earn "points" for teaching others what they know, and use points to learn from others. Harvard Business Online used a new model for its first course, disruptive strategy (ironically). Instead of the usual in-person model whereby a professor (or assistants) marks student assignments, learners are required to give feedback to each other. An exemplar assignment result is shared afterward for self-evaluation. Automated quizzes reveal the right answer(s) and why other answer(s) were wrong – making quizzing an effective learning tool over evaluation quizzes that just give a score. This and the multimedia platform enable learning to be delivered at scale.

Lesson: Learners can be harnessed as evaluators and provide a broader array of feedback than just one expert. Exemplars from masters and learning-oriented quizzes that share why an answer was right or wrong are also effective tools for learning and keep learners engaged. Employing both frees up teaching time to coach and to give feedback and evaluations on learning outcomes such as projects – or time to design new experiences. Automation and sharing the teaching role with learners can lead to either better quality interaction or scale – or both.

Gnowbe: Learning Communities and Microlearning

Gnowbe takes community even further by encouraging learners to post answers, outcomes, and ideas on community boards and share ideas, feedback, and invitations to collaborate. Taking a course or reading a "living book" on the platform is a far more social experience than individual online learning.

Living books, for example, can be continuously updated, making the materials "alive" (no second edition, like paper textbooks); they include prompts for learners to apply ideas to their own situations, bringing the ideas to life; and learners are encouraged to share with others going through the same materials, fostering connections, collaboration, and a living community.

As the world's first microlearning/authoring mobile-first platform, materials are personalized, participatory, social, accessible anytime/anywhere, and delivered in microlearning format – easy for busy professionals and bus-trotting students to access on the go. Information is presented in bite-sized chunks, aims to maximize learning in minimum time, and focuses on practical "hands-on" outcomes. Learning happens in short know-think-do-share cycles with short videos or readings, activities, and prompts.

As a result, learner **engagement is 10–15 times higher than video eLearning**.

Lesson: Learning in a social context is engaging and can be more effective, especially for social learners (remember the styles of learning?). Microlearning is a highly effective bite-sized and practical approach that gets people actively doing what they're learning about while they're learning. If you want to engage your learners or be engaged, or if you want practical outcomes from learning, this is a highly effective approach and platform.

WeLearn: Tech-Enabled Hybrid Mastery Centers and Personalized Education

WeLearn's mission is to bring affordable, personalized, future-oriented education to kids in emerging economies. It decouples place and program, offering "mastery centers" where kids in different online programs (accredited or non-accredited) can work alongside each other. They can also do tech-focused multidisciplinary projects (together or individually) in a physical, self-directed, mentor-aided mastery center.

Online programs are curated from around the world and included in the WeLearn platform. WeLearn Global includes both US and UK curricula, and there are over 5,000 specialist courses from John Hopkins University, Stanford, University of California, and many others.

It's like a physical, facilitated e-homeschool.

Student engagement begins with academic and socio-psychological assessments, and a profile is created of each student – the basis for designing a personalized curriculum. Customized digital tools are provided for pursuing a self-directed learning path, collaborating with other students, and peer mentor matching. A single dashboard depicts course progress and completion (even daily progress) across multiple content providers. It includes automated analysis, and ultimately, blockchain certificates. Mentors guide, assist, and monitor.

Students and their mentors design projects to explore various passions, apply learning, and fulfill learning goals. Tech facilities (and mentors) augment learning experiences with VR field trips, AR, collaborative holographic learning, interactive robotics, audio-video production studios, and a design and prototyping maker space.

I think they also have time for lunch and to make friends, too.

Loreto: Student-Led Teaching and Character-Based Education

What's the best way to learn? Teach, most would say.

So why aren't learners teaching? At Sister Cyril Mooney's Loreto Sealdah school, they are. Students teach part-time in village schools outside of Kolkata, India as part of their curriculum. They engage child domestic servants in play-learning and they lead learning circles in the school's Rainbow Program (initiated by a student), which houses street children and provides student-led education. The Brickfields program provides education in brick-making fields, where children live and work. Children don't have to come to schools. Schools can come to children.

Students not only teach but also propose new programs, giving them both superior mastery (as teachers), as well as skills in entrepreneurial thinking, service/program design, innovation, leadership, management, teamwork, social skills, and empathy – all essential skills for our technology-enabled future.

Sister Cyril's model integrates social programs and education. When she took over, the school had 700 paying students and a handful of non-paying. She purposefully grew the student body to 700 paying and 700 non-paying students, embedding integration into the business model.

She also integrated different social groups and engaged learners' emotion, action, and intellect to develop the student as a whole person, including character – seeing beyond themselves and hearing and respecting others in their society regardless of status. Group learning is the norm, and the physical environment shows it. Groups work around tables, and groups are led by the oldest and second-oldest students.

Interestingly, the second-oldest in a group is the leader, supported by the oldest. Initially, when the leadership was reversed, seconds-in-command sometimes did not support the group well and were not groomed and supported for their leadership role. By having an older child provide leadership support (after having been a leader), the younger one is engaged and growing, and the still-younger team members are well fostered by the other two.

Learning at Loreto is not about just gathering data, information, and knowledge. Understanding and wisdom are emphasized. This has empowered learners with the ability to evaluate problems not through mere analyzing but based on sound values and holistic perspectives, with a robust understanding of the implications of their actions to themselves, families, communities, and society.

Notably, analysis, fundraising, and policy writing are not the first steps in launching programs. Where there is a need, they just do it – start whatever good that can be launched now, and improve and scale as they go.

Did they achieve scale?

Over 35 years of launching and running educational and social programs, Sister Cyril and her team have changed the lives of 450,000 people.

Lesson: Learners can teach – and learn better by doing so. Not only does learner-teaching encourage content mastery (as long as teaching quality and potential mistakes are monitored), but it's also a great way to build human skills essential in the age of AI. Beyond learning and teaching, learners need opportunities to find unserved needs, create solutions, prototype, launch new initiatives, improve, and scale.

If you're not delivering this sort of experience or educating the whole person, it's time to redesign the experience you're offering. If you're considering a program that focuses on material vs. one that focuses on the whole person, with opportunities to create and lead new initiatives, you might want to choose the latter. More of humanity's efforts will be focused on doing so, and it's a good idea to start now.

How to Communicate What We've Learned and Who We Are: Another New Model

One difficulty with character-based education – and skill-based, too – is representing character and skills. Instead of today's transcripts, a new approach would be to graphically represent personal style and map skills on top of it.

In the same way some schools are beginning to blockchain transcripts, a 3DMindPrint could be stored on blockchain. In fact, with meaningful color-coding, skills could fade over time (represented by fading colors), the way real skills do (e.g. my computer programming skills). Long-lasting skills (like basic creativity or Design Thinking) and attributes could fade more slowly or not at all.

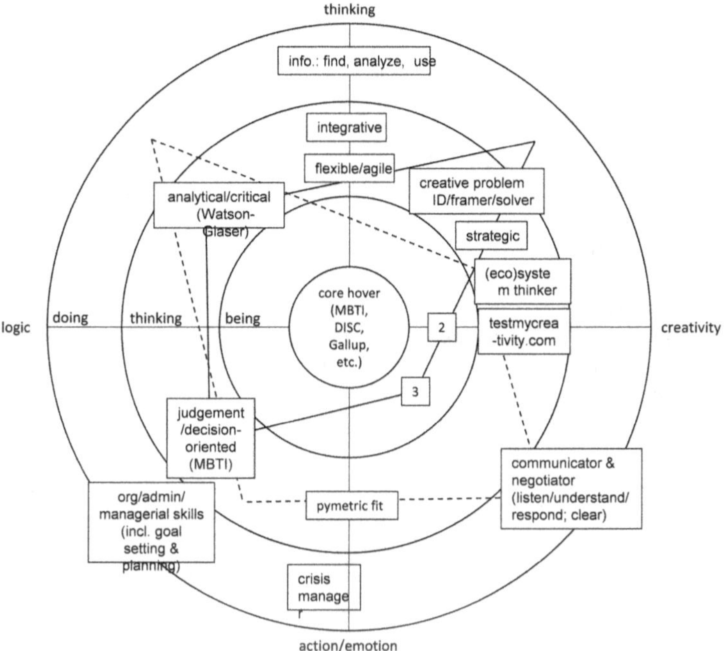

3DMindPrint: Reprinted with permission by *APAC CIO Outlook.*

I discussed a 3DMindPrint sample with a Learning and Development (L&D) friend at Google and explained that it could be based on HBDI, a psychometric test grounded in Nobel-prize-winning neuroscience. HBDI represents a person's normal style (solid line) and style under pressure (dotted line) across four categories – logic, creativity, higher-order thinking, and action/emotion.

Concentric circles could be shown for skills of being, thinking, and doing, per the FutureSkills framework above. Particular skills or a cluster of them (shown in the graphic as the numbers two and three) could be hovers. When you hover a cursor over them, more information can be given in the hover window while still maintaining the integrity of the overview.

You could share your MindPrint, and just like stacking HBDI profiles to see whether a team or organization is "whole-brained", MindPrints could be stacked to see if essential skills in a team or organization are covered or missing, yielding a team or organizational MindPrint.

Diversity and inclusion could also be fostered by including not only psychometric and skill diversity, but also gender, age, nationality, or other elements of diversity. AI monitoring could alert management to skewing and gaps, and AI hiring could be employed to fill in the gaps. In essence, an organization could develop an emergent consciousness and become (at least in some ways) self-aware.

Teams, organizations, and even nations are already attempting to characterize the workforce, for hiring, workforce planning, and national-level programs in education, as well as to attract foreign investment. Examples include European Qualification Framework (EQF), India's NCrF, VET, ESCO, Canada's Red Seal program in trades, and the European Credit System for Vocational Education and Training (ECVET).

National standards are compared in order to ensure parity across geographies for cross-border learning and work. Data privacy standards are necessary, especially when sharing information across borders, and national boards can also incentivize standardization via accreditation, awards, cross-border certifications, grants, low-cost loans, recognition, and tax credits.

Attribute and skill standards are essential so MindPrints (and other skills-tracking systems) can be compared and stacked, as long as we don't over-standardize and demand certifications excessively. We should include skills learned not only in formal education but also those learned via work, internship, and volunteer experiences.

Germany's dual-track vocational training program (VET) is a good example. It integrates job-based practical learning in the national curriculum and certifies over 500,000 apprentices annually. India's National Credit Framework (NCrF) assigns credits for academic *and* experiential learning.

Recommendations for Students, Educators, and Investors

Students

Be aware of what you need to learn for tomorrow, despite the fact that many programs you'll encounter are based on learning for yesterday's marketplace. Take charge of your own lifelong learning and make a plan, albeit taking advantage of government and employer support, where available. Finally, explore different learning models and pedagogies. Don't assume you have to go to a traditional school to gain qualifications. Consider learning experientially, and search for programs that'll give you "credit" for it.

Educators

Consider adopting a new model for the future and new (and old!) learning methods like those above, for helping your learners grow and succeed. Since education is ripe for disruption, any innovative model, pedagogy, or system could scale up quickly and become a competitor you hadn't anticipated.

Also, don't try to do it alone. The more seamlessly you integrate with employer and national systems, the easier it will be for your learners to be recognized, hired, and supported.

Investors

If you've invested in a traditional educational institution, find out how they're adapting to the new skills needed for tomorrow. Push for new (and old!) methods, facilitated by new technologies. Find out how management will leverage the existing brand, organization, systems, and customer base in the face of new competitors inside and outside what you both think of as the "education industry". Encourage them to use open innovation to partner with start-ups or spin off new, disruptive ventures, if they've not already done so.

Seek out new players who are custom-designed to support learners for the future, enabling themselves with advanced technologies, and envisioning global scale. Not every one of them will be a winner, but you don't want to miss the ones that will be.

5 New Business Models

The Internet produces new business models and also reinvents traditional business models.

–Marc Ostrofsky

Most companies are built to execute today's business model, not discover tomorrow's.

–Scott D. Anthony

Education is an odd business. Students are the input, the product, the worker, and the customer. Recruiting-companies are also the customer, buying the student-product.

The business model until now has been pretty simple – charge students fees so they can become input, perform work, and emerge a more refined product. But there are new business models we can adopt or incorporate.

DOI: 10.4324/9781003340713-5

When eBusiness first began, we only had two business models – value creation inherent in using this new channel and "eyeballs", i.e. brand awareness and marketing revenues from attracting people to a platform. Now there are over 20 eBusiness and revenue models that have been successfully applied across industries.

If we use the new business model in education, is there a way to make education more affordable – or even pay students to go to school instead of charging them? Yes. This chapter outlines not only various business models that could be applied to education but also a particular model that could make business education free.

"Unpacking" what schools do can also yield efficiencies by breaking up what individual schools do today so specialists can achieve economies of scale, deliver better quality, and enable consumers the flexibility and modularity to choose exactly what they want.

What If You Got Paid to Go to School?

One of my favorite business models in any industry came from a mathematics incentive program (see Jebara, 2017's TED talk). Parents pay, then students earn back the money by doing their math schoolwork (yes, it is work, after all). It isn't pay-for-performance. It's just pay-for-work, and better performance generally follows.

That got me thinking about the work students do. In general, they're exposed to new ideas, methods, tools, and skills. Then they practice with exercises. Then they tackle a real situation, in the form of a case to analyze, a project to do, or (in the case of business schools) sometimes a challenge or project for a real company.

Companies benefit from these collaborations. So why not share the business value created with the students directly? In some cases, small awards are given, but usually only a token, in comparison to the real value.

Instead of paying for performance to the "winning" students, another approach is for business (or any organization) to pay the school (commensurate with the overall value provided) so all students benefit in a collaborative manner and learning can be more affordable for everyone.

Beyond pre-defined projects, students could operate like "web crawlers", which find things on the internet. After exposure and exercises, students could "crawl" through an organization looking for ways to fix what's wrong and pursue new opportunities. Findings can become the basis for new project proposals.

Traditional schools follow the manufacturer's business model – we make and sell (albeit with components from others, such as books, articles, and cases). The revenue source (unless government provides funding) is student fees, and there's one value-enhanced product – the student. When students decide to pay (or parents, on their behalf), they carefully consider the Return

Table 5.1 Overview of Value Creation and Revenue Streams for Schools

Value Created	*Revenue Stream*	*Who Pays*	*Potential Partners (Sample)*
Individual learning and certification.	Traditional (albeit smaller) course and certification fees.	Learners.	Big-brand schools online, curated into hybrid programs (online material, in-person experiences).
Individual learning, transformation, and advancement.	Executive (and non-executive) coaching and education.	Lifelong learners, via subscription model (or today's per-service payment).	Companies like Epitome, which diagnoses people for job matches in the marketplace, matches them and recommends specific educational programs for potential job/career matches.
Corporate recruiting.	Future-of-workforce planning, selection, and development. In fact, companies are increasingly hiring teams ("acquihiring"), so placement activities could also be conducted for whole teams (not just individuals).	Company receiving new workers (note: one big-name consultancy in Singapore stopped hiring from universities and began hiring straight out of secondary school. They train new hires themselves or via online programs. Davis College in Hong Kong has companies "hire" people into their two-year diploma program. At the end of the program, the student goes to work. They're doing so well they're planning expansion to ten countries in the next ten years).	Deloitte's Future of Work Center of Excellence has a digital-future-workforce planning tool and would be a great partner for a school offering workforce future-skilling. Epitome (as above) connects people to job opportunities and needed training. Xopa.ai provides AI-based recruiting, and functionality could be added to include suggestions for needed training.

Corporate innovation.	Open-innovation projects.	Company receiving innovation services.	Companies, angels, venture capitalists, and innovation or entrepreneurship networks like TiE, IBM Garage, Found8, and Deloitte's innovation labs.
Social innovation and corporate CSR.	• Open-innovation social entrepreneurship projects • Corporate social responsibility (CSR) consulting to improve the department, make CSR more impactful and achieve greater synergy between CSR efforts and business outcomes	Impact investors; Gates Foundation, Rockefeller Foundation, and other social-innovation funders; corporate CSR teams.	Asia Venture Philanthropy Center (AVPN), BoP Hub, National Volunteer Philanthropy Centre, Deloitte's Unleash Lab.
Corporate consulting.	• Problem-finding via benchmarking, "audits" or "MBA Crawlers" who take newly learned frameworks/ approaches and apply them to a business • Diagnosis, problem-solving, and recommendations	Company receiving consulting services.	Big-name or boutique consulting firms.

on Investment, weighing both time and money invested and the resulting increase in their earnings (or other value-enhancement such as entering a new field). Value-added is shared by the student (maybe parents, too) and the school.

However, **if we create value beyond individual learning, this opens new possibilities for additional revenue streams and cost-sharing**.

Why not create a fusion of school, shared innovation center, consulting company, and incubator? A key component of each of these is learning, and the value each creates offers great synergy.

An overview (from the school's perspective) of value created and potential revenue streams is listed in Table 5.1, including who pays and potential partners. Because additional value is created beyond the traditional model, and because more players are contributing, the burden of education cost should be much lower for the individual learner.

The mission of a central organization (a "learning and innovation center") that creates value for the above stakeholders (partly through untapped synergy among them) might be: we help people, businesses, and societies grow.

In essence, a "school" can use a variety of new business models (including those outside education), such as the sample below:

- **Nickel and dime** (example: Ryanair) by charging for individual services instead of full-fee-full-service
- **Brick-and-click** (example: Sephora) with hybrid experiences
- **Retailer** (instead of manufacturer), using a curated selection of other schools' offerings (e.g. MOOCs), combined with in-house facilitated experiences
- **Low-touch** (example: Ikea products) and/or **high-touch** (example: installation services and custom curtains at Ikea), as chosen by individual learners and corporate clients
- **Subscription** (example: Netflix) for materials-only access or for becoming part of the "innovation community", with a specified set of benefits (e.g. number of events to be attended or hosted, number of projects to receive or take part in, etc.)
- **Freemium** (example: Dropbox) for service-samplers or alumni (some services for free, additional benefits with subscription)
- **Aggregator** (example: Airbnb), by using ecosystem members to provide mentorship or additional offerings
- **Agency** (example: Ogilvy) or **benefits-sharing** for consulting services (i.e. we search for value for free and keep part of the value we build with you)
- **Affiliate or network marketing** (example: Lifewire or Amway) for ecosystem members to recruit others

- **Crowdsourcing** (example: Wikipedia) could be built into the innovation and new-venture experiences, resulting in a growing knowledge base of experiences/cases (especially important to ward off competitors, who cannot replicate the growing knowledge base)
- **Data licensing/data selling** (example: Twitter) on an aggregated basis could become part of the diagnostics and biometrics used in programs
- **Advertising and commissions** could be part of the scene, e.g. for computing and electronics, travel, etc.
- And if the ecosystem succeeds well, it could be **franchised** elsewhere (example: The Hub new-venture ecosystem in San Francisco, which operates as a node of franchised nodes)

What impact might these new business models have on the traditional student-paid price of education? I've listed in Table 5.2 a host of elements you could choose to incorporate into your new model of education, alongside the potential impact of each on student fees, making education more affordable and – with many of the features – also better quality.

Unpacking the Program: Open-Sourcing Courses and Recognizing "Life Experience"

When I entered my 350-student lecture hall on my first day as computer science faculty (teaching accounting, of course) way back in 1996, I couldn't for the life of me figure out why students didn't just watch a VHS series of the best accountant in the world. Schools around the world could avoid paying expensive faculty by just buying a set of videos.

We no longer have VHS tapes, but my question remains.

Academics publish textbooks, simulations, and cases with teaching notes, and schools around the world buy them, then require professors to design and deliver their own courses. Why not sell whole multimedia courses and let students advertise on CVs and LinkedIn their branded certificates, in addition to their branded degrees?

In fact, I was talking with a best-selling author colleague from a big-name school who created a multimedia course based on her in-person course and was called into her dean's office. The dean wanted to know why she would package up a course from their fine school and offer it online. She shared that the online, low-touch experience she was extending to business executives was not the same as the in-person, high-touch experience, but still the dean would have none of it. She asked if they'd prefer she publish a textbook instead, and they said that would be great.

How exactly is a printed (or Kindle) textbook with accompanying videos and teaching/learning materials different from an online course? I still don't know. Nor does she.

Table 5.2 New Business Model Features and Fee Reduction

New-Model Features	*How It Could Lower Student Fees*
Payment by businesses for innovation projects and consulting, including • Problem finding via benchmarking, audits, or "MBA Crawlers" • Diagnosis, problem-solving, and recommendations (traditional consulting)	Corporate payments can fund part of the cost of running the organization (an "innovation and learning community"), instead of relying solely on student fees. Students work on real-life value-creating projects instead of only unpaid projects and exercises.
Payment by businesses for • Future-of-workforce planning • Employee recruitment/selection (including team hiring) • Development (learning) services	Again, corporate payments fund part of the cost of running the school. Corporate training is transferred from company to school (reversing the sad trend of education moving from educators to corporate centers).
Payment by foundations, impact investors, and corporate CSR (perhaps also governments) for • Social impact projects • CSR consulting to make CSR more impactful and achieve greater synergy between CSR efforts and business outcomes	Again, these payments fund part of the cost of running the school. Students work on real-life value-creating projects instead of only unpaid projects and exercises. We see an example of this today in government-funded educational institutions, which charge lower fees than private educational institutions, because governments pay to develop the society. Also, "live projects" for real organizations provide experience that learners can add to their CVs and LinkedIn.
Business outcome sharing for open innovation and consulting projects.	Value-based sharing to supplement (or as an alternative to) fee-based company revenues (again, revenues to supplant student fees).
Incubation and investment: fusion of school, shared innovation center, consulting company, and incubator.	Beyond the above, the community can generate wealth by generating and investing in high-value start-ups. Older educational institutions build up endowments, and in this age of start-up value-creation, why shouldn't a business educational institution build an endowment faster than ever before, from both individuals and invested enterprises? Endowments routinely provide scholarships.

(Continued)

Table 5.2 (Continued)

New-Model Features	*How It Could Lower Student Fees*
Alumni subscription for access to lifelong learning materials and events, e.g.: • Unlimited, subscription-based access to curated learning materials (videos, readings, audio, etc.), potentially to include internal/external platforms such as Gnowbe or edCast • Subscription-based access (with small event fees) to ecosystem events • In other words, freemium (like Dropbox) for alumni (some events for free, additional benefits with subscription)	As above, additional revenue to the organization, supplanting the need for student fees.
Subscription (like Netflix) for curated materials-only access, from non-alumni.	As above, additional revenue to the organization, supplanting the need for student fees.
Payment for certification without learning.	Lower cost. Why pay for education if you only need to take the test?
Payment for learning without certification.	Lower cost. Why pay for testing if you only want education?
Distribution of teaching activities from faculty-expert-only to faculty, industry experts, peers, and community.	Lower cost through volunteering and peer engagement.
Choice of coaching/mentoring via face-to-face (F2F), Skype/Zoom, or automated (e.g. via digital twin).	Lower cost by paying for only the level of service you want/need – F2F (high cost), Skype/Zoom (lower cost), or automated (lowest-cost for people who don't need hand-holding).
Use of MOOCs and automation of what we teach today.	Lower cost by using best-in-the-world materials already developed for other audiences. Lower cost through automation/pre-packaging of the organization's offerings, instead of delivering everything F2F.
Per-unit choice of online-only, blended, or F2F.	Choice of lower-cost online-only delivery vs. higher-cost blended vs. high-cost F2F (this can also raise quality via convenience).
Choice of best-in-the-world units (from Coursera, edX, HBX, Singularity online, IDEO.u, etc.) and best-of-the-school's units (from the school's own research and thought leadership).	Choice of lower-cost units vs. higher-cost (this can also raise quality via choice among best-in-class offerings).

(Continued)

Table 5.2 (Continued)

New-Model Features	*How It Could Lower Student Fees*
Customizable online dashboard only, Skype-based executive coaching, or in-person coaching.	Choice of lower-cost guidance vs. higher-cost.
Customizable level of automated tracking/reminding/escalating.	Lower cost through automation.
Easy online scheduling for coaching and mentorship and learning events.	Lower cost through automation.
Mentorship • By experts (i.e. faculty/executive coaches) or by community members, • Per unit or to include an overall learning coach • Learners also may choose and regularly interact with their own personal board of advisors • Business model: aggregator (like Airbnb), by using ecosystem members to provide mentorship and receive rewards/services in return	Choice of lower-cost vs. higher-cost options. More effective advising by self-choice and active engagement (which may ultimately be lower-cost).
Ability to earn "points" as a coach or mentor, to redeem for units, certifications, events, projects, etc. (i.e. a learning ecosystem marketplace).	Lower cost through the use of community members and non-cash marketplace instead of student fees and faculty-only.
Automatic issuance of blockchain certificates, diplomas, and degrees.	Lower cost through automation.
Automated recommendations of educational programs • To qualify for particular jobs (Epitome already does this) or • To receive diplomas/degrees (i.e. if you take these additional units, you would have this degree) • As long as you're in the ecosystem (potentially life-long)	Lower cost through automation, enhanced revenues through intelligent marketing and lower marketing costs (both of which lower reliance on student fees).
Online diagnostics, as above (coaching optional) of talents and styles for team selection, career/life choices, and goal-setting.	Enhanced effectiveness, which ultimately should mean more effective corporate teams/projects (as above) and learner outcomes (so enhanced revenues overall and lower reliance on student fees).
Full-time, part-time, and self-pacing (not everyone in a unit must finish at the same time, but obviously group experiences would finish together).	Lower cost by allowing people to earn money from jobs and "gigs" on their own schedule. Part of the cost to learners is opportunity cost – the need to quit their jobs to take a program. On the other hand, some want to use education to explain "CV gaps".

(Continued)

Table 5.2 (Continued)

New-Model Features	*How It Could Lower Student Fees*
F2F experiences may be short-format (e.g. for corporate execs who travel in for a long-weekend experience once a month or for one week a quarter) or extended (e.g. teamwork during new-venture building). F2F experiences could be attended by learners who know each other and are on a degree journey together (a cohort) or include some attendees who are joining only that particular experience.	Choice of lower-cost vs. higher-cost delivery and timing that suits the learner's workplace schedule.
Online, searchable alumni and corporate-ecosystem platform.	Lower cost by attracting people to subscribe to services/platforms such as this (i.e. additional revenue beyond student fees).
Pre-program job placement (larger companies can do this, especially those that already have integrated work/learn entry programs).	Lower placement costs since people are placed at the beginning of a "program".
Affiliate or network marketing (like Lifewire or Amway) for ecosystem members to recruit others.	Lower cost of marketing and enhanced revenues.
Crowdsourcing (like Wikipedia) could be built into the innovation and new-venture experiences, resulting in a growing knowledge base of experiences/cases.	More effective projects (so growing revenues) and a growing competitive advantage through the knowledge base, resulting in less reliance on "student fees".
Data licensing/data selling (like Twitter) on an aggregated basis could become part of the diagnostics and biometrics used in the programs.	Additional revenues and less reliance on "student fees".
Advertising and commissions could be part of the scene, e.g. for computing and electronics, travel, etc.	Additional revenues and less reliance on "student fees".
If the ecosystem succeeds well, it could be franchised elsewhere (like The Hub new-venture ecosystem in San Francisco, which operates as a node of franchised nodes).	Additional revenues and less reliance on "student fees".

That said, some schools are embracing this educational outsourcing idea. Harvard Business Online's CORe course is used by some universities instead of delivering the core business topics themselves – and students are happy to add Harvard Business Online to their qualifications. To encourage students to take charge of their own learning and offer a broader array of up-to-date topics, SPJ Global has students choose from an approved list of topics on Coursera as part of their curriculum.

Life and work are also important sources of learning to acknowledge. Through "life credit", some schools recognize workplace learning, broaden the learning packed into their degrees, and ensure practicality of student skills.

In Indonesia, university students can now choose to work in a start-up for a year and, if approved by the dean, get a year of university credit towards graduation. The skills learned are valuable not only to learners but also to a nation that seeks to foster an innovation and entrepreneurial culture (and ecosystem) for economic growth.

Unpacking Learning and "Passing": Certifications

Beyond unpacking the source of learning, learning and certification can be delinked. After all, to become a Certified Public Accountant (CPA), licensed attorney, or enter certain other professions, a college degree isn't enough. Certification is earned based on study for standardized exams, with or without a formal program, "prep school", or tutoring.

When I got my CPA and Certificate in Management Accounting (CMA), I bought a book to prepare for the exams and studied on my own. When my kids got their IGCSEs and A-levels, they used a curriculum and tutoring (i.e. homeschooling).

In short, there is a role for structured learning programs, and there is a role for standard certification and testing – but you don't need them from the same organization, and they can be delinked and individually scaled.

In fact, you don't necessarily need both at all.

Unpacking Learning and Space: Co-Learning Spaces

It's heartening to see schools reach out to each other for exchange programs, giving students global exposure, or joint delivery based on their relative areas of excellence, e.g. the accelerator challenge by Babson College (a leader in entrepreneurship), which admits students from other unis around the world to collaborate in teams.

One of the most innovative models I've seen takes this a step further and operates learning spaces similar to WeWork. I dearly wanted for my own kids in Singapore a WeLearn (based in Bangkok), which provides a safe, comfortable place for learners, no matter what school they're going to. They also facilitate social interaction (something homeschoolers and online learners struggle with) via optional activities and events.

At WeLearn, many students go to various online schools or use self-study programs, and they have a place to be – with others learning, growing, doing projects, socializing, and more – instead of being stuck in a room at home.

Any start-up entrepreneur or writer can tell you it's helpful sometimes to sit among other people in a "buzzy" coffee shop. My son often joins me in my office, because he simply finds it conducive to his studies to be among other people focused on their work. Unlike a library, food and drink are allowed, and with good reason – people want to drink coffee and eat snacks while they work.

Learning Marketplace: Choosing What to Learn, Your Coach, and More

What might all this unpacking lead to? In future, we may see an Amazon-style learning marketplace, in which learners can choose courses, coaching, psychometric tests, certifications, test center services, and more, with all the features of Amazon, such as five-star ratings, reviews, and more.

In my case, I used an online service and curriculum for my kids while they were homeschooled, but I had to search long and hard to find approved testing centers, some of which required overseas travel. A marketplace might at least have made the search easier.

My Kindle library lists everything I've bought and allows me to categorize them. A learning marketplace could feature different ways to graphically represent who I am and what I've learned, in a sharable way. Coursera, EdX, edCast, Gnowbe Learn, and others have made a good start, but I'm looking forward to a one-stop shop with all the features of Amazon.

Recommendations for Students, Educators, and Investors

Students

Although this chapter offers business model ideas for educators that you don't control, you need to be aware that there are different models out there and understand their impact on you (and your wallet).

You'll want to search for flexible programs that will allow you to make choices and avoid paying for what you don't need. You'll also need to be on the lookout for things like "life credit" so you can get credit for the skills you build/built while you've been earning a living. Having an option to gain work experience during a program is also valuable for learners who want to enter the start-up world, don't have experience, or again, those who need to earn a living.

Don't forget the option of studying on your own and showcasing the discipline you developed along the way (not everyone can do that). It can be far cheaper, faster (instead of marching in step while others learn what you already know), and offer a testament to a future skill: self-development.

Educators

There are a lot of business models and features above. Sift through them and consider which ones you'd like to incorporate into your organization and educational design. If you choose a radically different underlying model and set of features, consider spinning off a new entity with a totally new educational model.

Investors

If you've invested in an established educator, sift through the business models and features above with your investee and consider whether to add any to the existing business. Consider launching spin-offs with radically different models and features while leveraging the existing brand, core systems, marketing network, customer base, etc. For your EdTech spin-offs and start-ups, help them explore the various models and features and diversify the revenue base. Consider, also, funding an Amazon-type education market (perhaps with Amazon).

6 Enabling Technologies

Technology is just a tool. In terms of getting the kids working together and motivating them, the teacher is the most important.

–Bill Gates

Why are enabling technologies addressed here, after needs and business models?

Because technology, itself, is not inherently disruptive. It's an enabler.

Yes, we believe robotics and GenAI will enable and precede disruption, just as technologies like the steam engine, electrification, telephone, and light bulb enabled and preceded the industrial revolution. With new, breakthrough-level capabilities, we're on the edge of the next revolution.

But we have to **use** tech in ways that create radical value in order to revolutionize how we live, work, and learn.

When talking to groups about this, I often flash up on a big screen a picture of a man with a sledgehammer about to hit a car. He was demonstrating that this amazing car, built from bio-plastic, has fenders that dent and then can be instantly popped out. The vehicle ran on biofuel, and audiences generally say they're excited to learn more and use this great new innovation.

DOI: 10.4324/9781003340713-6

Surprisingly, the man in the picture was Henry Ford, demonstrating his new hemp car in 1941.

Why would such a great set of technologies and a great design not be an impactful innovation?

Because no one cared – at least not in 1941.

Sustainability was not a big deal back then, and with a world war having loomed on and then crested the horizon, it faded into the background, to be dusted off and used another day.

Even "soft-tech" (methods) enabled by "hard-tech" (hardware and software) face the same problem. I was super-excited about global telecommunications and computing enabling virtual teams, which I believed would spread around the world and foster economic growth and opportunities for millions. I was so convinced it was the future that I wrote my doctoral thesis on it.

Too bad it was further into the future than I realized. No one in the early 1990s had access to Skype or Zoom (founded in 2003 and 2011, respectively), and most companies didn't care to employ proprietary networks to work in this new way.

But when COVID-19 hit, people cared very much.

Even when people care, they often use technology for operational reasons and don't realize the strategic opportunities it opens up. Airlines, for example, employed technology to speed up once-manual bookings and make them accurate. Afterward, they realized it could be used for pricing and yield management, enabling airlines to maximize seat revenue according to booking lead-time and additional features such as the ability to change flights. Revenues rose dramatically. Online check-in was installed for operational and quality reasons (to reduce long lines in airports and enhance customer experience). It was only later that companies realized they could charge for seat selection and other services, now providing significant sources of revenue in a climate of razor-thin margins.

So, having begun our journey to education's future with needs and wants, then considering different approaches to making offerings viable, what new technologies will be key to making it happen? Are they ready today – or soon?

According to IDC (Anonymous, 2023), the real elephant in the room is GenAI, and I'll address those issues in their own section, below. But it's not the only technology important to education. In developed markets, within the next five years, we're likely to see more:

- Personalized, adaptive teaching by AI, focusing on complex real-life problem-solving
- 5G innovation hubs and "classroom" 5G use, enabling more immersive lessons, more out-of-classroom learning, real-time feedback, content access, and content creation
- 3D printing for tangible visualization and physical learning
- Digital transformation (DX) learning methods and skills upgrades for faculty

- Operational digital transformation, including
  - Scheduling systems
  - Security
  - End-to-end cashless payments for tuition, materials, endowments, etc., and
  - Blockchain records of skills, qualifications, and experience
- Omni-learning marketplaces

This is not an exhaustive list, nor are the sections below. They're just a highlight of the key technologies that have captured my attention and that deserve to be considered.

Quite a few technology enablers are mentioned in the above chapters, e.g. online material delivery and online human diagnostics, which may include psycho-neuro testing. Learning units in the future may include significant use of technology, e.g. biometrics for intra-personal development and interpersonal synchrony, or EEG readings for leadership coherence (i.e. whole-brained thinking). Cognitive and hormone tracking with biofeedback can also be conducted, to assess cortisol (stress hormone), serotonin (happiness hormone), and dopamine (reward hormone, useful for learning). Biometric monitoring can be performed with wearables during facilitated sessions or 24/7.

Chatbots can be trained to assist coaches during their sessions, similar to chatbots assisting customer service and sales professionals. Eventually, when bots become more independent, they can be released online to provide independent assistance to the whole learning community (of course, with access to humans as needed). Today, these are being evolved into sophisticated, mass-scalable tutor/teacher bots. The security and privacy of these multi-user, internal/external systems will be essential, as well as certification validity.

It's an exciting time to be exploring, experimenting, and employing technology in new ways.

Obviously, ICT, Internet, Multimedia, Simulations, and LMS

"Distance education" leaders like Open University (OU) have been around for over 50 years. Their systems were later placed on the internet, and the convenience and cost advantage of online education is undisputed. OU even collaborates with the British Broadcasting Corporation (BBC) to mass-distribute educational programming (or "edutainment").

Convenience is also a feature. Registration is online and integrated with both system forms to fill and human conversations. Payment is online, materials are accessible anytime/anywhere (and sent via post in paper format), dashboards are clear and functional, assignments and feedback are submitted online, and help is available through a variety of channels. OU tutorials are during UK timing, which poses a problem for synchronous interaction worldwide, but many students now use ChatGPT as an anytime/anywhere tutor.

They're doing something right to have amassed over two million alumni.

Multimedia and video-based learning materials (especially useful for audio and video/visual learners), simulations (super-useful for active/kinetic learners), virtual whiteboards (mural.co is my personal favorite), Zoom, and back-end learning management systems (LMSs) have all made education more accessible, impactful, and affordable. Google and Microsoft have created infrastructures for learners and educators and continue to enhance (e.g. with AI functionality) their education platforms.

Now, if only they'd put curricula and materials on the platform for the 250 million kids around the world who don't have a school. Curricula and materials do not a school make – but it would be a start.

SPJ Global's Engaged Learning Online (ELO) and Engaged Learning Centers (ELC)

There is one key problem with online learning – the 40–80% dropout rate and poor student engagement. In a bold move to make online learning engaging, SPJ Global launched a series of TV-studio-like ELO studios that make online, real-time learning experiences more "real".

Faculty and students make eye contact, interact with each other, have breakout rooms and polls, see names clearly (not the case with F2F backbenchers, even with nametags), and unlike in Zoom, learners appear in the same spot on the screen every week and throughout class time, facilitating relationship development.

Faculty are tracked as they move around the room teaching and face a wall-sized set of screens with 70+ students displayed, plus a content/drawing screen, chat screen, polling screen, signals to speed up or slow down, and more. When faculty takes a poll, students' name banners change color to show how they responded, facilitating discussion. Sessions are recorded, and students can search for what they missed due to inattention or simply need to go over again.

The video that introduces the technology (available at drcjmeadows.com/speaker and on YouTube) had to be kept short so didn't include a key surprise at the end of the case discussion. The case-company CEO logged in from Heathrow Airport to comment on the discussion and answer questions about what's happened since the case was written. That sort of interaction is golden for learning.

In short, benefits include:

- **Engagement**, facilitated by eye contact, real-time interaction, relationship development (people don't move on the screen or week-to-week, and names are easy to read), breakout rooms (using far less time than physical breakouts), polls, drawing, chat (which introverts and quiet cultures especially appreciate), and immediate faculty feedback from students

- **Always-on videos**, making each session feel **more real and personal**, unlike common practice in Zoom (turning screens off)
- **Global access** for learners (especially useful for traveling executives) and real-time classes including participants from around the world (global perspectives on class issues)
- **Less work/life disruption and lower cost** by eliminating travel (although hybrid programs can include face-to-face (F2F) workshops)
- **More guest speakers** because they don't have to travel, making learning more "real" and up-to-date

Thankfully, they launched their first studios (a first-in-Asia innovation) before COVID struck. The software that runs the systems is proprietary, and they've proved so engaging and enabled so many working professionals to get MBAs without disrupting their lives, that the EMBA program grew exponentially. New partnerships have also been formed to use it in executive education and events. They've installed more of these proprietary studios around the world to meet demand.

Are they more engaging? Yes. When scheduling conflicts force classes onto Zoom, students complain that it's not as effective, and they want the ELO experience.

Does this mean the school's F2F classes are less engaging than the tech-enabled ELO? No, functionality is also built into the multimedia- and internet-enabled physical classrooms (ELCs). ELCs also feature biometric attendance, emotion/attention sensing, and more.

Blockchain

Whether online or offline, once learning is achieved, credential security is critical, and handling transcripts is a time-wasting, automatable task. SPJ Global, for example, issues blockchain-enabled certificates (since 2019), and the use of blockchain for certificates, degrees, and transcripts could save a good deal of time and expense for most schools and learners.

Gnowbe: Microlearning, Social Learning, and Lifelong Learning

More people now have access to a mobile phone than clean water (Casey, 2016). So why shouldn't at least one educational platform be built mobile-first for mobile learning?

Gnowbe was. It delivers education in a micro-learning format whereby learners access bite-sized information and apply it immediately. It's used in corporate settings for onboarding, L&D, and ongoing learning needs as people work, as well as in traditional education settings. Although designed mobile-first for learning on the go, it is also accessible via laptop with a web interface.

Materials are easily entered and kept up-to-date, and the GnowbeLearn library is a publicly accessible, subscription-based repository of course materials and engaging experiences, as well as a place for learners to interact with each other – answering questions, giving feedback, and connecting for collaboration. It's not a replacement for Learning Management Systems (LMSs) like Blackboard (BB), but it makes learning active, engaging, and accessible anytime/anywhere.

I published my Design Thinking multimedia book on Gnowbe and integrated it into my F2F course and executive education workshops. Quizzes and marked assignments are submitted on BB, and published articles are provided via BB (which I don't propose we abandon). Everything else is Gnowbe materials, including a companion book for people taking workshops with me – plus human interaction.

It's worked well.

There are no lectures, except those provided as Gnowbefied videos, and those videos are the edited-first, best versions, making the online materials superior to what I would deliver on a classroom stage.

Our sessions together are spent on live projects and in-person exercises, making our time together more human and productive. We let tech do what it does well, and the unstructured work and leadership/coaching is provided by a human.

Although not designed for real-time sessions like the ELO, Gnowbe has been used effectively for conferences and events, including presentation materials, real-time polls, and more. It's especially effective for 30-day conferences that combine offline learning and group interaction with real-time experiences (either F2F or online).

Behavioral nudges are especially important for driving real impact and behavioral change after an event (e.g. training or a conference) and are delivered via the platform. Groups can also continue to interact with each other, and it's an easy way to share photos of their time together.

Benefits of the approach include:

- **Engaging format** – instructors can easily include videos, text, audio, links, reflective questions, polls, Q&A, and more (and update them continuously), and micro-learners are **10–15 times more engaged** than learners in traditional formats
- **Gauging engagement** – Did your undergraduate uni know if you bought the textbook? And actually opened it? And how much time you spent reading it? How many exercises you did? Gnowbe does that – one of the cool advantages of EdTech
- **Students can interact** with each other on the platform, fostering **peer learning**
- **Super-useful for flipped classrooms** – Any lecturing faculty would do again (for the 5,000th time) can be put on video easily and watched

by students. Classes then can become project workshops and coaching sessions with faculty, which students have told me is much better than lectures. Case discussions can still be held as usual, but instead of a printed case given on BB beforehand, Gnowbe can host video cases (via an external link if you don't own the video), and the "B" and "C" case continuations (especially if they are videos or online links) can be released during class instead of handing them out (on paper) during class

- **Publishing and marketing** – Multimedia textbooks can be produced with relative ease, and free introductory versions of an institution's courses can be hosted on GnowbeLearn for their 80,000+ corporate subscribers. This gets the institution's brand in front of an audience that may lead to executive education or degree admission. Authors need some instruction on micro-instructional design, but that's useful for engaging learners better, anyway, and a course on Micro-Instructional Design (MID) is available on the platform, itself
- **Offline access** of materials, where the author allows downloads
- **The educational organization keeps the data** (with an enterprise license), enabling data-based decisions
- **Student presentation handover time-savings** – I've just started requiring presentations to be hosted on Gnowbe instead of PowerPoint and found huge time savings since each group comes to the front of the room, logs in on the existing tech, presents from the online platform, and logs out. There are no problems arising from people using their own software and settings, having to lug their computers up to the podium, then finding the audio-visual setup doesn't work for them, etc. After 24 group presentations in a row for DT, I can verify that this savings is significant
- **Lifelong learning updates** – Wouldn't alumni love to see updates to a course they've taken, to help their ongoing L&D journey? Now they can. Alumni alerts can be issued when a course is updated, just like getting a software update alert. This helps keep alumni close, as learning community members, and fosters relationship, not just educational transactions

Pymetrics and Psychometrics

I was an early user of Pymetrics, which offered online neuro-psychology games, created a neuro-profile of the user (cognitive, behavioral, and social attributes), and then matched him/her with others who were successful in various fields.

It wasn't meant to mandate that you enter the field you matched best, but rather to open up possibilities you may not have considered. It confirmed fields that had been a good fit for me during my career and suggested some I might pursue in my then-50 years of time I'd probably have left on the planet. (Yes, I come from very long-lived stock so will need to learn and work for quite a while yet.)

I spoke with the Founder-CEO to find out if it would work on kids. Although the scientific studies to validate the approach didn't include minors, I went ahead and used it anyway for my kids, and it was terrifically useful for opening up new studies for them to pursue in new fields they hadn't considered.

Then their business model changed, and it became a platform for employer-employee matching and development, now focusing on the public sector. Potential employees can practice and even improve their profiles before interviewing with various organizations and take interview tests designed by Pymetrics for those organizations.

So why am I sharing a capability that's no longer offered?

Because the science is still there. It may have been the wrong time for Pymetrics' original offering, but perhaps they or someone else will offer it again. It's an innovative approach I found super-useful.

Nonetheless, other psychometric tests have also proven useful and are embraced by employers and employees alike, including:

- Hermann Brain Dominance Indicator (HBDI)
- Myers-Briggs (MBTI), and a free version is available, called 16 Types
- DISC
- Ikigai
- eParachute.com
- CliftonStrengths, from Gallup
- Basadur Innovation Profile

Not all of them began with AI. Myers-Briggs dates back to World War II, when there was a shortage of men to work in factories, offices, and elsewhere because so many of them went off to war. Women entered the workforce in millions all around the same time and had no idea what kind of work they should do.

A mother-in-law/daughter-in-law team (Mrs. Myers and Mrs. Briggs) stepped in with a psychometric test to provide guidance to those millions. There have been debates over the succeeding years on its accuracy, validity, and usefulness. And yet millions of people worldwide still use it for themselves, their teams, their organizations, and even personal relationships (it was very useful to my husband and myself!) so people can figure out their own style, appreciate others' differences, and figure out how to work together.

If a test has been useful to others and can give you a jumpstart on that, why not use it?

Psycho-Physical Tracking (Hormones, GSR, and more) and Neuro-Leadership

One of the leaders in the field of neuro-behavioral research in organizations is the Mind Brain Behavior Hive (MBBH) at University of Toronto. MBBH is a research, development, and design hub that aims to bring wearable computing, physiological sensing, AI and ML, and brain science into education and organizations.

They use not only neural activity and physiological responses (e.g. temperature, heart rate, respiration, Galvanic Skin Response (GSR), electrodermal, and electroencephalogram readings) but also synergistically use facial expressions, gaze shifts, pupillary dynamics, gestures and body language, postural kinematics, and voice characteristics for human development. Work is underway on digital phenotyping and using physiological readings to take an "emotional temperature".

Why go to this much trouble to sense a human?

Because people can't always tell you what they're feeling, how it differs from others, and how it impacts their behavior and "success". For example, a speaker or negotiator is more effective when they're "in synchrony" with others in the room. Learning how to synchronize with other people and synchronize others to yourself is a key interpersonal skill for the future. Learning how to manage your own intra-personal state is also a key FutureSkill (see framework in Chapter 4).

Stanford created a vision of the future of learning that included hormone tracking because various hormones can facilitate or inhibit L&D or simply alert us to a problem. These include cortisol (stress hormone which can indicate the mind is no longer open to learning and exploring); serotonin (happiness hormone which can indicate we're in the mood to learn and explore); and dopamine (reward hormone which can indicate we're succeeding and getting addicted to a learning game).

Psycho-physical technologies are useful for other learning situations, too. One study used GSR to track "anticipatory feelings" (AF) and correlate them with guessing-game success. By comparing traders who practiced prayer and meditation with those who don't, the researchers found (1) higher AF scores (i.e. more intuition) in the prayer and meditation group, and (2) higher profitability. GSR helped the researchers track and measure "intuition" and could be used in future to help people build and harness their intuition for measurable success (Hamelin & Boneli, 2022).

In another study, biometrics, eye tracking, facial expressions, GSR, and heat maps were tracked while people read stories. Emotional stories changed people's attitudes more immediately, but cognitive stories led to more long-lasting change (Hamelin et al., 2020). Educators or rehabilitation counselors (or marketers!) might use a similar approach in future to encourage and measure attitudinal change.

One of the most important uses of neuro-readings (available with an easily applied neuroheadset) is for decision-making. The researcher mentioned above (Nicolas Hamelin) leads SPJ Global's neuroscience lab and is pursuing neuro-education for leaders. His research found that better decisions result when more of a person's brain is used, supporting the assertions that "whole-brained thinking" leads to better decisions and innovation. In fact, using more of your brain at a given time is called coherence, and it can be tracked and trained.

Jill Watson, The Empathetic Tutor

Georgia Institute of Technology introduced an AI tutor, among human tutors. Students were not told the tutor was AI. They were only given her name – Jill Watson – which should have been a hint that she was part of IBM's Watson AI and data platform (especially for computer science students!). When feedback came back on tutor effectiveness, the AI tutor was shown to have done a good job.

Surprisingly, she got the highest score in something we assume is human – empathy.

When Digital People™ and digital twins are created, they are actually given personality traits, and some of them, e.g. curiosity and conversationality, can be experienced as empathy. Psychologists have identified three types of empathy:

- Cognitive – the ability to understand from another's perspective,
- Emotional – sharing the feelings of others, and
- Compassionate/Active – reaching out to help

AI enacts the above to varying degrees. These systems are normally trained with a variety of materials produced by humans, and ChatGPT (for example) can be asked for outputs in the style of a first-year undergraduate or a professional in a field, or even to take one side in a debate. So, it can adopt different human perspectives and can produce questions and answers appropriate to different personas.

AI currently cannot share human feelings, so that one's out. However, it certainly does provide help. Perhaps in the future, the ability to diagnose when someone needs help and then reach out to offer it can be added to the help it provides.

Why is this important?

Because Digital People™ and digital twins will probably be employed in roles that require sensitivity to others, e.g. counselor, tutor, teacher, coach, etc. In fact, they already are, to a limited degree. I have a digital twin (see Digital Twins section below) for teaching/coaching/assistance, and world-leading coach Marshall Goldsmith just announced his marshallgoldsmith.ai digital coach.

AI, Generative AI, and ChatGPT

Resistance is futile.

–Borg, Star Trek

Although the Star Trek protagonists facing the human-technology hybrid Borg did defeat them (so resistance was not futile), resisting technology in general is both futile and wasteful. Resistance fails to leverage a great new resource.

In fact, the Borg have already invaded (just kidding – only AI), and they're so quiet you may not realize they're there. Around 77% of our devices already use at least one AI-enabled feature (HBS Publishing, 2023).

I spoke with an executive from Squirrel.ai, one of the first companies in China offering large-scale, AI-powered, adaptive education. At the time, they had only developed math education at the primary school level, but they had already achieved a 1:3 student-teacher-ratio level of effectiveness.

What will happen when everyone starts to use it? What will happen when other topics are added?

Imagine the impact on private tutoring, which is currently a $45 billion industry in Asia Pacific set to grow at 8.4% – if AI doesn't take over that growth (Stellar Market Research, 2021). Imagine the impact on government schools in the most populous nation on earth (India), some of which have a 1:100 teacher-student ratio? Imagine the impact of providing such a service on mobile phones for the $250 million kids who face a 0:x ratio (i.e. no schools).

Beyond industry impact and serving more learners, scaling up impacts the AI engines themselves. With more data and more human interactions, the engines just get better and better.

Beyond AI in general, the giant in the room is GenAI. It strikes at the core of teaching and learning. The following sections on technology are useful, but mostly for advanced markets. GenAI today is free to everyone who can get a mobile phone and internet, and it awakens the possibility of the Socratic method again – teaching with questions and guiding learners in a more personalized way.

I'll talk here specifically about ChatGPT because it's the one I work with the most and is so popular with students (because it's free). However, it's not the only GenAI. My current favorite for research is Perplexity, since I can see its sources (easy for me to then read), put in better search parameters (e.g. include only sources after 2022), specify academic articles only (if needed), and set it to open ai (for information I don't mind sharing) or closed ai (for confidential or sensitive information).

Other tools produce text, images, text-to-speech, and more, such as AlphaCode, DALL-E, DreamFusion, LaMDA, Stable diffusion, Whisper, etc. GenAI content writers include CopyAI, Jasper, Rytr, and others. What I say below can be applied to many other GenAI systems.

One weakness of GenAI (at least currently) is lack of semantic logic and understanding, as well as belief. Try it out. Ask it if it believes something it's just told you. It declares that it's an AI language model and states that it doesn't have personal beliefs and opinions.

It tells you what others have said, but it doesn't evaluate what it's telling you. That's your job.

Case in point: don't do what my CEO-friend's intern did. She asked the CEO to sign a reference letter for her upcoming job search. Not only was the letter so generic it would be useless and unread, but it got her gender wrong! She hadn't even read her own reference letter.

Assuming the user is awake and paying attention, GenAI opens up the possibility of personalized learning interactions, reviving the Socratic method. That said, without an innate drive to evaluate, understand, pursue truth, guide you to better questions, and probe for logical or semantic consistency, it isn't replicating Socrates' conversations.

It's a hollow imitation, albeit better than nothing, and useful for prompting humans to pursue truth and understanding.

Google's work on semantic search not only gives us better searches, but perhaps it points the way to enabling Large Language Models (LLMs) like ChatGPT (or their own systems) to evolve into semantic LLMs.

For more information on human understanding, the Socratic method, and rhetoric, I recommend videos and books by Professor of Law Ward Farnsworth. If we're learning in order to take action and persuade others to take action (the original meaning of rhetoric: persuasion, not just talk), we need to persuade others to believe, and we need to believe, ourselves. Our systems will be more effective if they believe, too.

Final note on belief: ChatGPT is able to admit mistakes, and as users become increasingly aware of the need for critical thinking and verification, users can correct and teach CGPT, learning well in the process because the best way to learn is…? To teach, as the saying goes.

Before delving into how to use ChatGPT for education, I should probably address a couple of questions:

Did I write this book without ChatGPT?
Of course not.
Did I have ChatGPT write this book?
Of course not.

First of all, I'd surely get in trouble with my publisher for plagiarizing, if not ChatGPT, then the sources it learned from. (And any student I've punished over the years for plagiarizing will come haunt me.)

Second of all, ChatGPT doesn't generally ask itself great questions (although that feature may grow) – at least not the questions I (and probably you) want answered. As with Design Thinking a product, a reader has needs or desires they want satisfied. Even if ChatGPT or a designer thinks up something really cool but not needed or wanted, it'll be tossed aside. So, don't bother. I, the author need to ask questions for you and write for you based on my deeper understanding of you.

Third, as you've probably noticed, this book is a personal conglomeration of ideas and anecdotes from decades in the education business and homeschooling, as well as an as-yet-unpublished framework. It's not something ChatGTP could write because it's personal.

I asked ChatGPT to make a framework of skills important in the future of work, and it gave me a top-ten list (actually, it cheated a little by combining some skills). These are included in my framework, but my framework also graphically represents them (for us visual learners) and includes a deeper message than just top-ten, with interplay among the elements (see FutureSkills framework above). Here's ChatGPT's list (paraphrased, reordered, and edited):

1. Adaptability and resilience
2. Creativity and innovation
3. Critical thinking and problem-solving
4. Cultural competence
5. Data analysis and interpretation
6. Digital literacy and technology skills
7. Emotional intelligence and interpersonal skills
8. Entrepreneurial mindset
9. Lifelong learning
10. Teamwork and leadership

I use ChatGPT to meet a better class of people.

– Dr. Chris Marshall, VP Data Analytics and AI, IDC Asia Pacific

GenAI is a wonderful research assistant, essential these days since human research assistants have gone the way of secretaries and woolly mammoths. You rarely encounter them anymore (although we do have executive assistants and elephants). GenAI scours what's known, so I can include and build on it.

What about ChatGPT for education?

Basically, it's today's calculator.

Educators had to adjust to the use of calculators instead of manual math and, as long as students could understand the basics of numbers and their relationships, they moved on to using the new tech and developing higher-order cognitive skills.

It became more important to judge the reasonableness of a calculation than to actually calculate it.

Same with GenAI. Some educators have ChatGPT write an essay and then ask students to evaluate it and build on it. This is what students will have to do in the workplace and whenever they consume news reports. Not only have many news reports been written by AI for years, but we're seeing the rise of bot media personalities like Lil Miquela (2.9 million followers), Guggimon (1.5 million), Knox Frost (1 million), Noonoouri (404,000), and Bermuda (263,000).

With so many people enjoying H2R (human to robot) interaction – which can be real-time 24/7 and individually customized – will these same humans be satisfied with a less engaging, less real-time educational experience?

I think you know the answer to that. (No need to ask ChatGPT.)

Some changes to today's education will be necessary in this new GenAI world. For one, assessment needs to change from evaluating a report that ChatGPT can write to:

- Oral exams/evaluations
- Exams/evaluations that focus on complex issues, problem-solving, and higher-order thinking, not just fact regurgitation
- Multimodal outputs instead of just exams and reflective papers – audio, video, graphic, physical (e.g. prototype), and in-person (or video) presentation. That said, VALL-E can produce highly realistic audio with a three-second voice sample. Make sure you're evaluating your student, not an AI representation of him/her!
- The quality of questions asked, not just answers (note: we now call questioning "prompt engineering")
- Classroom/workshop interaction
- Discovery and debate
- How well students synergize and create with their tools
- Collaboration with both humans and tools
- Project work, including the process, not just the outcome
- Real outcomes that can be used to make people's lives better
- Staged assessment, in which you evaluate learners during the process of writing or creating something
- Research evaluation, e.g. assessment of evidence; identification of assumptions; and review of methodology or lack thereof
- Human-oriented skills in the FutureSkills framework

Beyond plagiarism and modes of evaluation, concerns abound regarding using GenAI, including bias, inaccuracy, and overreliance on AI instead of creativity, investigation, critical thinking, and interaction with experts or peers. For plagiarism, I use tools like SafeAssign (embedded in BB), which alerts me to both traditional plagiarism and AI writing detection. GPTZero is also available.

To be honest, students can take a GenAI essay, translate it into another language, and then translate it back to English (in my case) to escape automatic detection. But they can't fake our human interaction and real-time work together.

I've had students turn in GenAI-written reflective essays on our experience together, with personalized experiences added in. Unfortunately, the only writing that appeared to be original was mainly wrong. Sadly, students who plagiarize to pass a course often can't even do that right.

So why not let GenAI enhance work and learning by producing properly attributed bullet points, computer code, emails, essays (or other writing), formatted references, graphics, poetry, presentations, reports, secondary research results, social media posts, tables, tweets, and videos – to name a few?

It can even provide your desired tone (so add this to your prompt if you want a tone), including academic (I don't generally use this one), authoritative, descriptive, formal, friendly, funny, informal, persuasive, professional, etc.

It's also worth exploring the many plugins that are available for accessing scientific literature, data and video analytics (including transcript generation), interacting with the internet inside a ChatGPT conversation, writing and sending emails (which my digital twin can also do), and more.

In short, here's my top-20 list of good uses of GenAI for learners and educators (which I wrote after experience with it and reviewing quite a few articles for ideas – not just asking ChatGPT):

1. **Familiarizing and attuning** yourself with advanced technology (remember: tech synergy itself is a key future skill)
2. **Learning/improving language, writing/referencing, editing/formatting, and conversation**. Since I haven't chatted with Chat GPT to learn a language, my personal favorite is reference-list formatting. Not only is it a chore I hate to do, but I usually do it wrong or with an outdated format (despite Googling the format and examples)
3. **Overcoming writer's block** e.g. producing potential introductory sentences to choose from
4. **Researching** what's known about a topic (research assistant), not only for the sake of your research but also to enable smarter conversations between learners and educators, making their time together more productive

5. **Tutoring, explaining**, and producing "explainers"
6. **Helping you learn by 80/20**, i.e. identifying the most important 20% of learnings on a topic to understand 80% of it
7. **Simplifying**, e.g. "rewrite the following so a beginner can understand it"
8. **Summarizing**, e.g. "from the following text, give me bullet points of the key insights and most important facts"
9. **Generating ideas and divergent perspectives**, e.g. listing ideas to approach a problem or accomplish something, or showing you different points of view in an argument
10. **Debating**, e.g. practicing a debate before you have one or improving a position essay
11. **Co-authoring or serving as a muse**, e.g. with Verse by Verse (part of Google AI, not Open AI), you can input a line of poetry, followed by the AI's contribution, and so forth. At some point, you can have the AI write the rest of the poem or offer suggestions in the style of famous poets
12. **Critiquing**, e.g. proofreading your writing and suggesting improvements, giving feedback on a mock exam, explaining something to ChatGPT to see if you got it right and communicated it well
13. **Producing writing for critique**, whereby learners (1) evaluate the question/prompt (remember: asking good questions may be more important now than giving good answers), and (2) examine assumptions, biases, alternative explanations, evidence, arguments produced by different AI engines, etc.
14. **Planning lessons** or refining or explaining plans you created
15. **Making discussion prompts**, e.g. crafting statements from particular perspectives to incite debate or exploration
16. **Creating exemplars**, i.e. sample outputs at different levels of mastery
17. **Producing activities**, e.g. creating exercises or projects "flipped-classroom" style
18. **Generating quizzes, exams, and custom cases (including practice ones for job interviews)** for discussion, practice, and testing, especially if you can include something local, recent, or based on your experience together. Apparently, ChatGPT has "limited knowledge" of post-2021 events (HBSPress, 2023) – now post-2022 – and surely this limitation will disappear as it learns to keep completely up to date. Nonetheless, it surely won't know what you've discussed and worked on in workshops together and haven't uploaded to the internet, unless we create systems to learn from what we're doing in workshops, real-time – which we may, for better human-tech creative synergy
19. **Crafting marking rubrics** for external examiners
20. **Updating learning materials**

Remember to attribute the AI writing and build on it (don't just use it and never think about what GenAI gives you!). In APA style, the in-text reference is (for example): (OpenAI, 2023). The references-list citation would be: OpenAI. (2023). ChatGPT (GPT4, Mar 14 version) [Large language model]. https://chat.openai.com/chat.

Don't just direct your learners to do that. Model the behavior.

And remember: time saved on "duties" means time available for learning and real engagement!

Example prompt[s] for ChatGPT you might find useful include:

> Write three college-level multiple choice questions that target key student misconceptions around how natural selection works. Include feedback for students.
>
> Design a marking rubric for a postgraduate assessment that asks students to apply their knowledge of the global financial crisis to a more contemporary economic challenge. The rubric needs to assess students on their use of literature, their analysis of the underlying causes of the GFC, and apply it creatively to a contemporary challenge. Please provide standards for each criterion from high distinction, distinction, credit, pass, and fail.
>
> https://educational-innovation.sydney.edu.au/teaching@sydney/how-ai-can-be-used-meaningfully-by-teachers-and-students-in-2023/

VR, Haptic Computing, and the Metaverse

When my daughter was 12, she became a coal miner.

No, not IRL (in real life) – in the metaverse (and with other elements and minerals, too).

On her own, she pursued making money (metaverse coins) with her mining efforts and then invested it in building a coffee shop. I don't remember whether it was Starbucks or non-branded. You can buy Starbucks franchises, branded goods, and lots of other things on various metaverse platforms. But on her own (no prompting from Mom), she built up and ran a successful business, serving other metaverse visitors with food, drinks, and a place to hang out.

What an awesome learning experience!

She also became a well-regarded gamer and streamer, collected money on PayPal for her streaming events, and bought things like a Meta virtual reality (VR) headset and a mod (a custom-designed model/avatar), both to enjoy and to further her craft and following.

Again, what an awesome learning experience!

Now that she's moved on to LinkedIn for job applications, she has transferrable skills in crafting an offering and building a business, as well as an understanding of how to build a presence and following online (e.g. on LinkedIn!) – and is a self-starter and self-developer (again, FutureSkills).

Medical and engineering schools have long been using 3D and VR simulations to help students try out new surgical skills and engineering projects which can be tested with complex models used in real-life sciences research and professional systems for structural computer-aided modeling.

Haptic computing is another great way to train new surgeons to perform procedures, via realistic practice and tactile feedback. It's also useful for rarely performed surgery – rare in general or for a particular doctor. After all, practice makes perfect (or at least patients hope it does).

Are such technologies useful for less-scientific disciplines?

Yes.

30 MBA students at Harvard Business School, for example, "visited" the homes and shadowed families in southwest India to understand more deeply their consumer needs in healthcare and wellness. Not only was it more affordable and convenient than F2F, but VR made the experience possible during COVID.

Some French business school students can attend classes, work as interns, perform research, access services, and socialize as avatars on a virtual campus. They can also interact with other students from around the world – with a minimum of disruption to their work, lives, and F2F classes in other locations (HBSP, 2023). ESSEC and INSEAD hold VR-based classes, and INSEAD uses VR in both degree programs and executive education. NEOMA created a completely virtual campus.

The metaverse has the potential to disrupt F2F learning just as impactfully as the first wave of technology disruptors, such as 2U.com, edX, Coursera, Lynda.com, MOOCs, Udacity, and Udemy. Instead of dissecting a case set in the past, the VR experience can be real-time and current.

Learning to be better decision-makers from the past is essential, but so is learning to make decisions and create new solutions today. VR and the metaverse enable us to do more experiential learning outside of classrooms, and including context in the learning experience enhances engagement, relevance, and effectiveness.

Is this important for corporate L&D?

Yes.

A PwC study found that VR-trained managers were 40% more confident acting on what they learned than those who were trained F2F in a classroom. Improvement over online learning was 35%.

Not only can students choose what to focus on in an immersive VR experience – unlike looking at curated PowerPoint slides – the system enables them to be a "fly on the wall" instead of changing what's observed with their presence.

Learners can enter car factories, semiconductor fabrication facilities, and more, packing in more visits per day (with no travel time) and interactions with on-site staff via avatars. Current problems, opportunities, and new designs can be discussed and even tried in real-time.

VR immersion can easily run again for a "do-over", and slow motion and zooming in are useful features – without disturbing the subjects of observation. If learners watch or participate in several different scenarios in succession (with no traveling across town, waiting for a different time of day or season, etc.), they can have a condensed learning experience and can use it before they make in-person visits. Approach and interview questions can also be refined before encountering interviewees. Further, comparing and contrasting the environment they're in with other nations enhances cultural learning, an important future skill.

VR can be used across the education value chain, from admissions to delivery to placements to alumni relations. During the admissions process, for example, students could tour the campus and get a feel for "a day in the life" of a student, including housing, class, study group, cultural events, guest speakers, and more. Classes and projects can use VR (see above), and the placements process could be enhanced with VR-based preparation and interview practice – and even VR interviews with key corporate recruiters.

For alumni, Harvard's Division of Continuing Education is collaborating with VictoryXR to launch a digital-twin campus. VictoryXR is a commercially available platform for single and multiplayer use at universities, K-12, and **even homeschooling**. They work with over 130 colleges and universities worldwide.

Spatial Computing, Holographic Professors, and Visual Wrap-Around Experience Rooms

Apple's Vision Pro has been lauded as the dawn of spatial computing, freeing us from devices on our hands, laps, and desks. Combining elements of augmented reality (AR) and VR, the operating system allows users to launch and use their apps with fingers and eyes, integrated in what they see immersively via headset, instead of fingers on screens, keyboards, mice, and touchpads.

Will it revolutionize education?

It'll certainly enhance it. Anything we perceive as taking place around us and that gives us a more "real" experience is inherently engaging and should make learning more "real", too. After all, learning is a combination of enhancing our perceived reality with new information about the past, as well as trying out new skills and versions of ourselves to enact a new future.

Holographic teachers (and speakers, meeting attendees, etc.) are another relatively new way of interacting. It's a step towards making long-distance interaction "more real".

Wrap-around experiences can also be used to create a realistic experience – or to immerse in something beyond reality. My personal favorite is my time in the Van Gogh Immersive Experience. With projections of painted surroundings on the wall, floor, and ceiling, it was like walking into a Van Gogh landscape – a trip to southern France, but better. The VR portion of the exhibit allowed me to walk through indoor and outdoor painted environments 3D-style and see everything around me – forward, backwards, left, right, up, and down.

Could such experiences be useful in education?

SPJ Global has a wrap-around room that gives potential students a feel for the cities they'll study in and the places they'll go. It could be used to help students practice TED-style talks, present business plans in a boardroom, and (if integrated with a metaverse environment) interact in real-time with c-suite executives in their offices, plant managers in factories, workers delivering goods to retailers, potential consumers solving their day-to-day problems, etc. – without a headset.

The one I'm waiting for is the Star Trek holosuite. Operating with holographic people and photons resequenced into matter, it's a more extreme version of a metaverse wraparound and won't be possible for quite some time. Nonetheless, the Star Trek characters offered a vision of a future when they used it not only for interactive novels and entertainment but also as a space to try out new skills and explore and develop new technological, scientific, and interpersonal possibilities.

Children learn by immersive play, and adults are no different.

Can we make future visions real?

Why not? We do it all the time.

One of my favorite examples – the flat-screen TV – was featured in Star Trek's "Requiem for Methuselah" in 1969, when only one-third of US households had a color TV, and the cathode ray tube (CRT) display was the dominant technology (filled with hazardous materials like cadmium, beryllium, lead, and mercury). Not until 1997 (28 years later) were the first functional flat-screen TVs introduced into the market.

My favorite example for the education industry is Apple's The Knowledge Navigator video (look it up on YouTube – it's six minutes well-spent). John Scully presented it in his keynote at Educom, the then-leading higher education conference. It featured an advanced and conversational AI professor's assistant with voice-recognition-enabled natural language processing, touch-screen tablet computing, AR, seamless connectivity across devices and systems, cross-database integration and analysis, multimedia features, and interactive learning and discovery via a highly interactive and intuitive user interface.

It aired in 1987 when I was developing green-screen online stand-alone systems using CRTs and a mainframe.

The only technology we didn't have at the time was the foldable screen (now popular on phones).

Why did it not take off back then as the world-changing technology of the day?

I can only guess that it wasn't commercially viable, and perhaps people didn't have a burning need to develop and adopt it. At least we have embraced such technologies now, as shown by our rapid adoption of GenAI assistants.

The big question is: what can we develop and adopt in 2024? 2030? 2034?

Who knows.

For now, I'm developing, adopting, and eagerly watching.

Harvard and SPJ Global Professor Bots

Harvard introduced bot teachers into their General Studies in Technology course and Introduction to Computer Science (CS50) – one that senses how you like to learn, what you already know, and what you need help with. It adjusts accordingly. Knowing that ChatGPT and GitHub Copilot would be "too helpful", Harvard created its own large language model.

Beyond helping students debug code, giving design feedback, and answering questions 24/7, it'll focus on leading students toward an answer instead of providing it. It hasn't replaced the professor – it just augments learning 24/7, essentially making the teacher-student ratio 1:1.

SPJ Global currently has a professor bot in development, based on the same technology as Ameca, the world's most advanced robot, including human-like facial expressions and body language. Ameca can mirror people's movements, sketch, and hold a conversation, drawing on ChatGPT and other AI. (For a seven-minute YouTube video, just google "Meet Ameca!".)

I wanted to offer my teaching videos to the SPJ Global developers so I could be a model to draw from, but since I help students discover and explore needs in the real world (which they'll design from) and focus on project coaching during unrecorded class time, there wasn't anything to work with. Interestingly, some other faculty who did work in recorded classrooms didn't want to contribute their teaching videos. My husband (a tech guy himself) advised against it, in case the technology would replace me.

In truth, the very thing I teach – Design Thinking – is a highly human skill, since we explore unstructured situations and generate small amounts of data AI can't (currently) work with. That said, I'm certain a bot teacher could help. We use GenAI when prototyping, and I'll discuss my tech teaching enhancement (a digital twin) in the next section.

Concerns over bot teachers include missing the "human touch", omitting social and contextual learning, reducing the need for human teachers, and neglecting human discovery and exploration.

These concerns can be overcome if we consider what humans and technology are uniquely good at and their limitations; clearly define their roles; enhance personalized learning and dynamic curricula; employ productively the faster feedback that tech offers; use humanizing elements like natural language processing and emotional sensing; discuss human issues like ethics and social impact; help teachers learn and stay up-to-date; evaluate and continuously develop the tech and its impact; communicate transparently; and foster synergy between human and tech teachers – each doing what they do best, plus achieving together what they can't do alone. We'll need to incorporate these elements in our day-to-day work and in our newly necessary bot-teaching policies (which Harvard had to introduce and which now extend to its EdX offerings).

Digital Twins

Digital twins are set for rapid adoption. … Like artificial intelligence a few years ago, digital twin technology has tipped from highly specific applications into becoming a widespread management best practice.

–CNBC

Companies have been digitally twinning assets (e.g. factories and buildings) and processes (e.g. factory production and energy systems) for some time, but most people thought digitally twinning humans would be decades into the future.

Happily, the future has arrived.

Soul Machines has been making Digital People™ since 2016, and they also make digital twins for celebrities and other prominent people like Jack Nicklaus. Digital People™ work in company "digital workforces" to help customers register for events and services (e.g. opening a bank account), receive wellness information particular to their situation, and more, in a personalized, empathetic way. Companies they work with include Google, Microsoft, Amazon Web Services, the World Health Organization, and others.

The moment I discovered an affordable, commercially available digital twinning platform that didn't require the help of an expensive development team of my own (personal.ai, which launched in 2020), I jumped on it (digitally).

I gave my twin (CJ2.personal.AI – I call her CJ2) personality characteristics like empathetic and conversational. (I had to turn off curious because she got too curious in her interactions). Then I fed her my books, articles, videos, and websites, and could have included meeting transcripts or videos if I wanted her to learn from meetings. She and I had some conversations to help her learn and to reassure me that she'd represent me well.

Talk with her!

She answers questions for my readers and students 24/7 and helps them think through applying Design Thinking, fusion (lateral innovation), sustainability, strategy, and other topics to their particular situation. There's no limit on the number of people who can interact with your twin until you hit the presidential level, and personal.ai is working with a country leader to overcome that issue.

How do I know she works?

My husband fights with her.

And others have told me she works well.

You can make several different personas with their own style defined by you, e.g. business leader, teacher, coach, and mom. The CEO of the company has a dad persona that interacts with his kids. A twin can be integrated into emails, WhatsApp messages, and more. Twin responses can be automatically delivered or merely generated for the original human to edit and send (it's a simple switch in the settings).

Currently, my twin has an interface like ChatGPT, but newly released platform updates now include audio, so I'm eager to have CJ2 learn my voice and inflection so people can talk with her. Video is in the works.

Although many companies prohibit the use of ChatGPT for work, because it learns and shares with others (it is an "open" AI, after all), personal.AI enables you to easily create your own small language model closed AI system.

Would a digital twin be useful across the education value chain?

Yes.

A marketing and admissions twin could provide personalized help during the search and admissions process. Delivery would be enhanced via 24/7 personalized help from a teacher twin, area head coach twin, dean twin, administrator twin, counselor twin, general school twin, or others. Students undergoing placement could have personalized coaching to help them obtain their best jobs. Alumni could receive coaching and mentorship for the rest of their lives on a paid or unpaid basis (e.g. as a benefit of the school, making the school a preferred educational option). Different tiers or subscription plans can be established.

EdTech and Testing Centers

The above technologies are exciting but not cheap.

Not every education provider has the information technology (IT) staff or desire (and budget) to invest in their own technology facilities. Even though proprietary systems can give an organization a competitive edge, technology is not the core function of most schools, and proprietary systems can easily fall behind what big commercial developers offer. (In fact, they often do.) Further, some educators will still want to test knowledge at key points in the learning journey with the aid of computing but without GenAI and other tools, so specialist centers can prove useful.

Unbundling technology from the organization could provide enhanced learning across the educational marketplace. As a homeschooler, I'm very familiar with testing centers for IGCSE and A-levels. The CPA exam, bar exam, and other tests are conducted in special centers. Online learners at all levels would benefit from the technological access and social environment a specialized center could provide.

There's undoubtedly an education-business opportunity for someone who wants to help learners and their educators access a full range of educational technology (EdTech). With the increase in independent learners, I predict, the opportunity should be both business-to-business (B2B) and business-to-consumer (B2C) in nature.

Recommendations for Students, Educators, and Investors

Students

When choosing a program to join, consider what kind of technology your educator will use in the education process and how both they and you will use them. You don't want to spend your learning and development time in an environment that's not exposing you to the best of today's tools and not preparing you for tomorrow's. Get familiar with the technologies above, begin using what you can (if you haven't already), and don't settle for less.

If you're going to create your own learning journey, start with your needs/desires, put together a viable set of options (financially and logistically), and seek out educational opportunities using the above technologies. Your CV won't look like the standard-qualified job candidates many companies are looking for, but it will portray you as having the FutureSkills companies are already seeking (and having trouble finding).

Educators

Consider integrating any and all of the above technologies into your existing offerings, and give yourself a chance to experiment with them. Some uses of tech will not emerge until you start "messing around" with them. A key lesson from Design Thinking is to "think with your hands" and "think with your feet", suggesting you not only experiment but also make a tour of other organizations that use these technologies. Get their perspective. Find out what's useful and not useful, what they discovered along the way, and shortcuts that may be available now but weren't around back then.

If you're designing new offerings, trawl through the above and consider the breakthrough capabilities they might give you and how you'd use them for your own competitive advantage and your learners'.

Investors

Trawl through the above with your current education investees, probing for whether they've considered using these technologies, experimented with them, or implemented them – and how they're evaluating, improving, and expanding their use.

You'll definitely want to do that with your start-up investees, and you'll want to scan the world for leading-edge use cases both in use and in development. Consider what breakthrough capabilities they enable and whether there's a market of people wanting them.

Don't shy away from using high-tech in low-tech, underprivileged circumstances. That's where disruption happens – at the bottom of the market – and a key feature of technology is to enable breaking through physical constraints, e.g. (in education) lack of qualified teachers and tutors, inability to travel or access physical resources that could be replaced with the metaverse, and more.

Remember to set aside some budget for your investees to experiment without constant pressure from you. At a minimum, you can build the brand with their push to be innovative. At a maximum, they'll eliminate expensive processes and achieve breakthrough capabilities.

Finally, think about the possibility of investing in an EdTech and testing center, B2B and B2C – or a network of them (franchised or fully owned). If fully owned, not only should the centers provide profitable cashflow, but you can also surround yourself with your own or others' affiliated businesses to serve your clients as they come and go. You might find yourself in McDonald's' situation, making money from the core business and making even more money from real estate in and around your locations.

7 Tales from a Homeschooling Parent

The Future of Primary and Secondary Education

People say homeschooled kids are too sheltered from the real world. At what point did sitting behind desks all day become the real world?

–Anonymous

As a homeschooling parent, I'd like to extend some of the above ideas to primary and secondary education and share some of what I've learned with those of you who are (or are considering) homeschooling, either as a learner or as an educator.

My husband and I moved around the world for professional and family reasons. In so doing, our four kids have been in:

- English-and-Mandarin preschool
- French primary school (conducted in French, of course)
- Kahn Academy home-studies in the interim between France and Singapore, to avoid six months of no school (since France uses the western school calendar and Singapore follows the calendar year)

DOI: 10.4324/9781003340713-7

- Singapore English-medium primary school for two kids, secondary school for one, and homeschooling for one who didn't gain admission
- Homeschooling for all four, supported by UK online school (a formal, accredited program) and in-person tutoring (since the UK timing for classes and tutors was at night in Singapore, where we lived). I worked full-time and part-time while managing our homeschool, which included six classes for four kids, so basically 24 learning projects (not a lifestyle I recommend)

Singapore has been ranked as the world's top English-medium school system. Unfortunately, it's available to very few expatriates, based on the three- to five-hour admissions exams that select only the very top students. Private schools are prohibitively expensive for many families, like ours (especially with four children).

I was startled when I realized that among the 250 million children around the world without a school, four of them were mine. Thankfully, my kids did not join the 300 million who apparently leave school unable to read and write (UN, 2023).

I was also stunned when I found that in Asia, it's common practice for kids to go to school all day, learn little or nothing, and then have tutoring during evenings and weekends, when they do their real learning. If they're learning from tutors, what's the point of the school?

The schoollessness problem, then, includes kids who (nominally) have a school.

Whether a child ranks among the world's poor or among the increasingly global middle class, the implications of schoollessness are enormous. Societies around the world need well-educated populaces and leaders for stability and economic growth. The growth of a disenfranchised class – the Precariat – could be catastrophic (Standing, 2014; Hanauer, 2014).

What's Available, and What Do We Wish We Had?

We used a number of solutions (listed in Table 7.1), each of which satisfied some needs but not all.

What do we wish we could have had if we could've integrated the best of all? For a vision of the future of education (including K-12), just go to the next chapter. The vision includes not only adult and "lifelong" learning, but also K-12, making the vision truly lifelong.

The vision does not call for an expansion of the welfare state but rather sees private organizations as drivers, using new capabilities opened up by technology. Thoughts on the above elements especially relevant for K-12, are included here:

Table 7.1 What Schools (and Non-schools) Provide a Child

Student Need	*Online Self-Learning*	*Online Accredited School*	*Homeschooling*	*Physical School*
A (Safe) Place to Be				X
Social Engagement				X
Curriculum Design		X	Some curricula can be purchased, but you'll have to evaluate them	X
Help Available When Needed		Somewhat (depending on the time zones)	X	X
Flexibility	X		X	
Progress/Outcome Checks		X		X
Quality and Certification		X		X
FutureSkills	X	?	?	?

- **A Place to Be** – Kids need a place that's safe, flexible, fun, and effective. Parents and students should be able to decide which days and times (if any) a child will attend in person. Kids can be tracked with GPS, with notifications given via mobile phone. They'll need quiet solo study places, group work places, and modular places for sports, music, and more. These might even be rented or shared with other organizations.
- **Social Engagement** – Kids trapped at home during COVID missed out on social learning and engagement, and kids in physical schools often miss out on global exposure. If online and physical platforms are available, kids can have the best of both.
- **Curriculum Design** – Project-based learning is engaging, effective, and appropriate for K-12. (See the overview of Lumiar in the New and Old Learning Models section in Chapter 4.) The capabilities to be mastered by graduation need to be set and tracked, but the path to mastery can be flexible and personalized.
- **Help Available When Needed** – Whether help is a student, teacher, "supervisor", "tutor/mentor", or community expert, and whether in-person or online (e.g. from an overseas call center), help should be available when needed. The internet, volunteerism, and community ratings (more stars for better helpers) make it possible and economical. Loreto students teach, ACE teachers are supervisors/coaches, and these can be supplemented with student communities who give feedback, help, and even marks to each other, in online and/or physical communities.

- **Flexibility** – With self-directed learning (especially online), not everyone needs to be doing the same thing at the same time in the same place or with the same learning style. With the ACE system, for example (as well as Kahn Academy), independent learners often move to the top of a course cohort; move down when they have trouble and spend extra time working through difficulties; then move up again. In the current army-like school march, when a kid has difficulty, he/she drops back (or out) and may never go forward again. Flexibility is needed for both pace, place, and program, and can be used and paid separately. Kids should be able to go to a learning center to work on a group project or just to study alongside other people enrolled in different curricula. Pricing models should also be flexible, including money and volunteering or other contribution(s).
- **Progress/Outcome Checks** – Some online educators use technology to ensure progression, e.g. when a video is played, a question is answered, then another becomes available and is not available until the prior is played and the question answered. Loreto and ACE, on the other hand, are paper-based, and progress is checked by a person (a Loreto teacher or student-teacher, and an ACE student or supervisor, as well as periodic self-checks). A global school in widely varying economic circumstances could use either material – paper or electronic. If a teacher has a phone, he/she can at least present ideas to students and draw on a chalkboard or in the sand. Wealthier locations short on teachers could use computers and call centers. Poorer locations that have teachers but no computers could use paper. Where libraries of books are not present and are too expensive to create, global NGO Worldreader can help. Since 2010, they've helped over 22 million readers in over 100 countries access books via the BookSmart and Worldreader apps for phones and Android tablets.
- **Quality and Certification** – Although accreditation of schools was originally put in place to close down diploma mills that did not teach sufficiently, the accreditation process can impede innovation with its slowness or by focusing on process checks and organizational issues instead of outcomes. In fact, accreditation rules are not always up to date with new processes and organizations enabled by new technologies. That said, in the above examples, Loreto is well-regarded and affiliated with the West Bengal Board of Education, and ACE issues a US-curriculum high-school diploma. In fact, I was surprised to find that admission to a good university does not necessarily require a diploma from an accredited secondary school. All the higher-learning institutions I investigated internationally accept outcome tests like GED, HiSET, or TASC from the US, or IGCSE and GCSE A- and O-levels from the UK.
- **FutureSkills** – Information search and scoping, problem framing, communicating, creating individually or by gathering resources (like teams), learning how to learn, learning through failure, and more are key skills for the future (actually, today, as well, but many of us get by with less).

> Will arithmetic and spelling be obsolete everywhere? No. Besides, there is some value in learning at least some "industrial-age" skills for convenience and brain-training. We just shouldn't focus all of a student's time on them. Because of the difference in skill-needs and circumstances, it will be important to customize for the individual economy and student and evolve what's offered. That said, some things considered futuristic, like learning how to innovate and launch new enterprises, are relevant for everyone. Tomorrow's schools should feature personalized, adaptive learning and customization, as well as materials improvement by the cohorts themselves.

Thankfully, my kids have become extremely adaptable – perhaps the most important capability for the future – seeing life from different perspectives, using different languages, in city and country, rich and poor, on different continents, with different education systems.

They and their schoolless counterparts are inventive and resourceful. Perhaps in this, they are advantaged, and the schooled children are disadvantaged.

Perhaps schooled kids would be better served by schools designed for the schoolless.

Recommendations for Students, Parents, Educators, and Investors

Students and Parents

Don't assume your local government school, private school, and staying home (an impossibility for most people, including me) are your only choices. Explore the models in Chapter 4 (How to Learn: New and Old Learning Models). Reach out to WeLearn and other organizations that can help you craft personalized journeys if the standard ones aren't working for you. Curriculum designers are available from a variety of organizations online, and if you don't find a personalized solution right for you, then you may have to cobble designs and services together on your own, as I did.

Further, consider offering to others what you do out of necessity, so they won't have to do the same. You may have a new job and a growing business if you do.

Educators

Put your Design Thinking hat on and investigate whether you're really serving your stakeholders well – students, parents, teachers, and community. By spending time with them where they are, asking questions, listening, and watching, you may discover unmet or underserved needs. Investigate the models in Chapter 4 (How to Learn: New and Old Learning Models) and go through a Design Thinking process to design and develop new or enhanced offerings.

If it's radically different from your business today, consider spinning it off as a disruptor.

Don't forget the learning styles – visual/spatial, auditory and musical, physical/tactile, verbal, logical/analytic, kinesthetic, solitary, and social. Make sure whatever you offer helps learners learn best in their own style.

Learners need to choose their context, materials, and activities to be optimally productive. Can you integrate that flexibility into your designs?

Investors

Work with your educators to investigate (design-thinking-style) how well-served – or not – their students, parents, teachers, and community are, today. Investigate the models in Chapter 4 (How to Learn: New and Old Learning Models) and help them both identify unmet needs and continue the design thinking process to develop new or enhanced offerings. Innovations that enhance the existing business should stay in the business. Those that are radically different (and hopefully disruptive) should spin off into new ventures.

With what you've learned, working with your existing educators (or learning about the future of education, if you're a start-up-only investor), help new offerings grow. To achieve global scale, some tech will be necessary, but don't focus only on the tech. It's an enabler. Focus on what needs will be served, how much scale and value there is in the problem, and whether your new offering will serve students, parents, teachers, and communities ten times better than today's solutions.

And don't forget to use new tech like GenAI to offer existing materials in the various learning styles – visual/spatial, auditory and musical, physical/tactile, verbal, logical/analytic, kinesthetic, solitary, and social. Solitary and social learners need to choose their context more than materials style, so work with your investees to design that into their offerings. Online social learners especially need a WeLearn-like context. With some publisher licensing, you'll find a large community worldwide of learners who want alternative-format materials.

8 Vision, Design, Launch, and Growth Options

We are limited not by our abilities but by our vision.

–Kahlil Gibran

As mentioned earlier, incumbent companies do not disrupt themselves. Their existing resources, processes, and profit model all work against the new venture, and incumbent executives have built-in incentives to kill a new offering that could cannibalize their part of the business.

That said, by having a new-venture investment group within your company, you can include a disruptive business/offering as part of the company's holdings. You wouldn't be the first company to see the old business shrink while the new one grows.

Final note before turning to the future vision: make sure your minimum-viable product is profitable **before** you scale it up. This may sound like dumb advice, but executives in resource-rich companies have more than once found it tempting to stick to the pre-arranged timeline, thinking they can work out commercial issues as they scale.

All they do is scale up losses.

So, start small, get it right, **then** scale the hell out of it.

DOI: 10.4324/9781003340713-8

Vision of the Future of Education: Fusion of the Best Designs, Business Models, and Technologies

Imagine a comprehensive educational ecosystem combining the most effective elements from traditional and modern learning models. This system would cater to both children and adults, blending personalized online and in-person experiences. It would include a global, adaptable, and community-centric learning environment, leveraging cutting-edge technology and social collaboration to enhance educational outcomes. By integrating key concepts from various pioneering models, this innovative learning framework offers a holistic, truly lifelong education solution.

Each learner would have access to the world's best online programs, integrated into a tailored, personalized educational plan, supplemented by physical WeLearn-type centers. These centers would provide a safe, social environment, some of which (where appropriate) would be equipped with advanced technologies like VR, AR, collaborative holographic learning, interactive robotics, audio-video production studios, and design and prototyping maker spaces. Solo study and group activities (e.g., projects, sports, music, drama) assist in fostering a cohesive learning community. In K-12, older students would mentor younger ones, enriching their own knowledge and character development, while aiding the learning process for younger learners. For all ages, community experts would also play a significant role by sharing their wisdom and skills, ensuring an age-diverse environment and diverse learning experiences.

Learners would start their educational journey with comprehensive assessments, including psychometric tests, biometric readings, and neuro-headset readings, guiding the formation of educational pathways for personalized development. This customized learner-plus-expert-led approach, inspired by Montessori, Lumiar, Stanford, and other models, begins with individual interests and integrates AI and human expert guidance to generate a personalized curriculum.

Learning materials would cater to various styles – visual/spatial, auditory and musical, physical/tactile, verbal, logical/analytic, kinesthetic, solitary, and social. For example, an audio-learning student would have access not only to textbooks but also to audio versions for improved retention. AI narrators simplify this adaptation, presenting opportunities for publishers to capitalize on new, high-profit formats of existing materials.

Incorporating the flexibility of WeWork, WeLearn centers could spread globally, allowing individuals and families to travel for pleasure or business or relocate for employment during educational programs without disrupting education. In fact, travel can be a terrific educational experience in itself and should supplement, not disrupt, education. Such setups would support family cohesion and community sustainability, especially as urban designs evolve towards smaller, green-infrastructure communities within larger mega-communities.

A learner's curriculum would emphasize FutureSkills and character development, using a mosaic rather than a linear timeline, much like Lumiar's model. This structure accommodates student-initiated, project-based learning and allows for AI-generated curricula refined through human coaching. Specific classes would be offered face-to-face when viable, with online alternatives involving regional or global cohorts. VR/AR and metaverse integrations would enrich these experiences where appropriate, while gamified and microlearning materials maintain engagement.

Tutors and coaches would be accessible on a per-use or subscription basis, offering both in-person and online support. Digital twins, developed on platforms like personal.ai, would offer 24/7 support. Assistance for special issues like ADHD, autism spectrum disorder (ASD), and counseling needs (among others) would be included in the marketplace, for kids and adults, alike.

A digital dashboard similar to those used by OOL, OU, and WeLearn would track mastery, progress, and estimated finishing times per subject and overall program, alerting learners and parents (or employers, if they're paying for a program) about achievements (great time for a reward!) and areas requiring help (including how to get it).

Centers could feature higher security for kids' areas, as well as less secure areas for adult learners. Buildings need not be custom-built. Schools, libraries, and other community buildings could be transformed into learning and community hubs, featuring quiet solo areas, group areas, technology facilities, and food, drink, social, music, sports, and other facilities in modular, repurposable designs. Traditional classrooms would be rare, if needed at all, since most people will listen to lectures on their phones and shift to project-based learning. Small and large performance areas would take their place. These new centers would also be used as innovation hubs for corporate, government, NGO, and community-based organizations.

Beyond traditionally qualified teachers, experts in various fields and learners themselves could speak, teach, coach, and mentor, in exchange not only for money, but instead (or in combination) for access to events, programs, and equipment (similar to Stanford's vision of learning communities). This interactive learning loop would solidify and enhance learning (best way is to teach, apparently) and encourage continuous knowledge sharing and innovation.

The use of neuro-headsets, biometrics, hormone sensing, and psychometric tools would remain central in understanding and guiding human development throughout each learner's journey. With the aid of progress-tracking dashboards, monitoring mastery, and signaling when additional help is needed, personalized curricula would be mastery-based, not time-based, allowing learners to spend more time when needed or accelerate as desired.

Learner-initiated projects would be supported by a project marketplace displaying opportunities from various companies, governments, NGOs, and others who provide support to (and benefit from) the learning-and-innovation ecosystem. Adult learners could earn well while learning, sharing the value they create for those organizations as they learn, contrary to today's pay-to-learn model.

Collaboration with organizations would turn these learning centers into innovation hubs, with learners identifying and implementing value-creating improvements. For example, "crawlers" could dig through organizations' practices to see if the "textbook" way of doing things is actually happening. While doing so, they would identify opportunities for value-creating improvements and submit potential projects to the project marketplace. Crawlers who find better ways than "textbook" can share (publish), so others can do something new and better – a learning-community learning loop.

Learners would have the option of exiting their workplace for an intensive experience or (more attractive for most) integrating work and learning, either continuously or for short periods of time, alternating between the workplace and learning space. They would have the option to continuously reskill and apply new learnings to their work.

Classes, workshops, and lectures (speeches, really) would be available face-to-face or online, with engaging, real-time interactions facilitated by advanced-technology platforms like SPJ Global's ELO studios (far more engaging than Zoom). Tutors and coaches, supplemented by AI and digital twins, would provide round-the-clock support. Progress and mastery checks would vary, as appropriate, including self-assessments (like ACE), automated reviews, and human evaluations from peers (like Harvard Business Online) and/or experts. In fact, self- and peer-assessment are important skills, themselves. Feedback on right and wrong answers can be automated for learning (like Gnowbe), and behavioral nudges can be delivered (again, like Gnowbe).

Courses should be available worldwide, operating as "plug-ins" to larger programs offered by others, the way specialized software "plug-ins" integrate with larger platforms like Outlook, Chrome, and Safari. This would be facilitated by standardized "transfer credits" and "life credits", easing the integration of global educational offerings.

Would schools still exist? Yes, education is an essential service, and curation and other elements of the service will still be needed.

How would they compete? Some elements will remain – brand name, social network, specialist experiences, and thought leadership – the latter of which may instead continue to separate into its own industry. The rest will change. As industries like education mature, and "interfaces" become more standard (e.g. "plug and play" courses like Harvard Business Online's CoRe, technologies that assist plug-and-play learning, etc.), businesses shift from a unified, one-stop-shop strategy to a modular strategy, competing on the basis of specific offerings, offered globally.

Education providers will need to rethink what they offer, modularize, specialize, and disintegrate (not necessarily disappear).

Learners could either follow a single institution's curriculum or cobble together courses from multiple sources on a globally accessed (Amazon-style) education marketplace, creating a personalized degree issued by third-party providers, thus unbundling space, learning, and certification/degrees. Degrees, diplomas, certifications (e.g. SCRUM for adults, IGCSE and A-levels for kids, etc.), and professional qualifications (e.g. CPA, the bar exam, etc.) would be issued with blockchain technology, ensuring security and authenticity. The tests themselves would be given on-site or online (where appropriate), with security features such as facial recognition, eye tracking, sound sensing, and other technologies.

Does this vision sound like a nightmare to manage?

Of course it does.

But that's what we have AI and other technologies for. The complexities already embedded in our intricate and interconnected global financial systems, marketplaces, logistics networks, healthcare systems, IT platforms, and transportation networks already surpass the above.

This vision presents not so much a "school" but more of a "learning ecosystem". It's a high-level vision, and the next step would be to design the marketplace, as well as for particular providers to design their offerings, e.g. courses, certifications, degree/diploma programs, prices, admissions/recruitment, progress tracking, delivery systems, and more.

Given the blended, community-based, MOOC-friendly, technology-enabled nature of the overall design (including corporate and any other funding to supplement student fees), the prices paid by individual students should be significantly cheaper – if not free or paid-learning for innovation and business-improvement outcomes.

Ultimately, this is a vision of a personalized, global, technology-enabled, flexible, market-driven, community-fostering, lifelong learning environment for everyone.

And as usual, technology isn't the problem. It's getting people to stop grinding out business as usual and serve needs in a new way.

One Sample Program: TechVenture LaunchPad

To give you a more concrete idea of just one small program that could be launched by an organization that wants to get its metaphorical toe in the water, here's a high-level design of a venture program that could be launched at a business school. You or your designers would need to add to it and do more detailed design, but this vision should give you a start.

Participants:

- Individual tech-venture aspirants (pre- or early venture, teams welcome)
- Family business leaders who want to launch digital products, services, or enterprises
- Corporate innovators and intrapreneurs developing digital products and services or new ventures

What They'll Get:

- Knowledge, skills, and tools in technology, business, innovation, entrepreneurship/intrapreneurship, analytical thinking, creativity, leadership, and self-development
- Branded certification in key skills
- Mentorship and coaching from experts
- Network/ecosystem

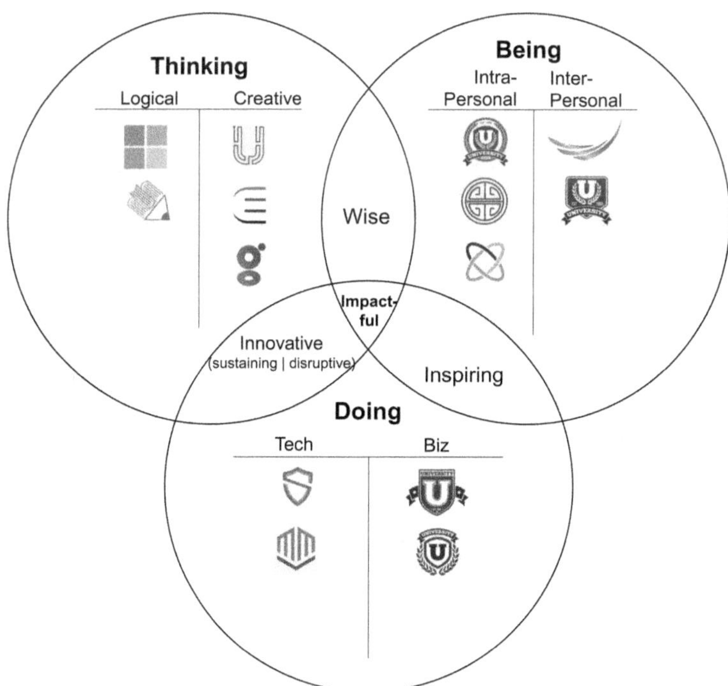

In the graphic, you'll see a variation from the above FutureSkills framework. The "Doing" bubble has changed from running today's business and creating tomorrow's to technology and business because new tech ventures generally focus on integrating technology and business. Depending on the nature of the business, the founders may not need so much focus on today's businesses. That said, if it's a B2B venture, it may be set up in order to change today's client businesses. If so, then the design should revert, and tomorrow's business should include a heavy dose of relevant technologies. Detailed design on what to learn about today's business will depend on the particular venture, so part of the design should include flexibility to accommodate the needs of particular ventures.

The "Being" bubble includes Berkeley's Science of Happiness online course, HBDI, MBTI, and the Center for Creative Leadership's course on Becoming an Innovation Leader. The "Thinking" bubble includes online courses such as Microsoft's Logic and Computational Thinking, IDEO.U's Unlocking Creativity, ExperiencePoint's Experiencelnnovation, and Gnowbe's Innovation Through Fusion.

The "Doing" bubble includes Singularity University's Foundations of Exponential Thinking, Harvard Business Online's CoRe and Disruptive Strategy, Stanford Online's Cultivating the Entrepreneurial Mindset and Scaling Excellence, and MIT's Startup Success: How to Launch a Tech Company in Six Steps.

After all, who wouldn't want to do a one-year program with certifications from Harvard, Stanford, MIT, Berkeley, and Microsoft – and have a viable enterprise at the end of it?

Features:

- One-year expert-coached program (as non-degree executive education while awaiting accreditation)
- Project-based, hands-on learning
- Multiple learn-do-reflect cycles during the process of developing a product/service/venture
- Participants learn plus apply learnings to their own product, service, or venture
- All knowledge-acquisition via MOOC, some paid (for branded certifications)
- Periodic web events (e.g. weekly, bi-monthly, or monthly) with quarterly F2F retreats – or fully F2F
- Panel judging by Funders (Angel, VC, private equity (PE), etc.) mid- and end-year

Partners:

- Offering institution (e.g. a business school)
- TiE (network of 15,000+ founders and funders worldwide)

- Mentor/coaches (technopreneurs, technologists, funders, c-suite executives, designers)
- edCast (AI "speed-learning" platform)
- Found8 or other innovation and entrepreneurship ecosystem hub for F2F events, co-working, networking, etc.
- IBM Garage

Learn-Do-Reflect and Do-Learn-Reflect

For the things we have to learn before we can do them, we learn by doing them.

–Aristotle, The Nicomachean Ethics

Each unit of learning during the program would follow a learn-do-reflect pedagogy, with possible "do-overs". Alternatively, the program designers could follow a do-learn-reflect cycle with "do-overs" since sometimes, people need to try it their way, see the results, learn a better way, then try again and reflect. Whichever approach is chosen:

- Knowledge transfer and exercises/cases would be online
- "Doing" would involve applying new knowledge:
    - To the learner's self, new venture idea, or existing job/business, or
    - To "consulting" projects (innovation and new-development challenges) from companies
- Reflecting can be done orally or in writing with a cohort (including peer feedback) and/or an executive coach/mentor

360-degree qualitative feedback would be given throughout learning experiences – and acted upon – including:

- Self-evaluation and reflection (e.g. against sample work/answers, progress toward personal goals, etc.)
- Peers and teammates (or the learner's workplace, for learning applied there)
- Angels/VCs/PEs (for innovation/venture "pitches")
- External approval (publications, media appearances, etc.)
- Facilitator/experts (traditionally the only feedback)

A coach/mentor can help the learner understand and process feedback and the overall developmental process. If the group is large or the program has grown, learners should be allowed to choose one or more coach/mentors. If more than one is chosen, it could act as a "growth board" or personal board of directors (see Stetler, 2022).

Modularity would be a core feature of the flexible learning system/ecosystem, with learners able to choose any or all of the following (each with its own price, enabling economy-access or premium-service, following the example of budget airlines):

- Unlimited, subscription-based access to learning materials (videos, written, audio, etc.), potentially to include internal/external platforms such as Gnowbe and edCast
- Subscription-based access (with small event fees) to ecosystem events
- Learning journeys and certification units paid per journey or per unit
- Interactive components (plug-ins, basically) that transform online-only, solo learning into hybrid learning (online plus F2F)
- Certification testing, paid per certificate, independent of unit-based learning – i.e. learning unit/journey/experience and certification would be priced independently, as EdX and Coursera do, so some people can take a course only, and some can take both. Unlike EdX and Coursera, in this design, learners with experience should also be able to take certification only, without the formal learning process, which they've already done via experience
- Choice on the learning platform of best-in-the-world units (from Coursera, edX, HBX, Singularity online, IDEO.u, etc.) and best-of-this-school's units (from the school's own courses, research, and thought leadership)
- Customizable online dashboard, including progress tracking and Lego-style graphics of units and the degrees/diplomas they can stack into, as well as comparison with self or other benchmark(s) like a "class average" (if desired)
- Online or F2F coaching
- Customizable level of automated tracking/reminding/escalating (for those who need automated assistants to nag them)
- Easy online scheduling for coaching and mentorship and learning events
- Mentorship by experts (i.e. faculty executive coaches) or by community members, per unit or to include an overall learning coach. Learners also may choose and regularly interact with their own personal growth board (personal board of advisors)
- Automatic issuance of blockchain certificates, diplomas, and degrees
- Automated recommendations of educational programs
    - To qualify for particular jobs (Epitome already does this) or
    - To receive diplomas/degrees (i.e. if you take these additional units, you would have this degree)
    - As long as you're in the ecosystem (potentially life-long)
- Online diagnostics (coaching optional) of talents and styles for career/life choices and goal-setting, including Pymetrics, HBDI, Simplex,

MBTI, DISC, testmycreativity.com, MPQ, empathy, learning style, etc. (note: the bundle could cost less than taking the tests individually if the school negotiates licenses at-scale). This is a baseline for experimenting/exploring to develop one's own most effective work methods, learning methods, and life/work goals

- Automated team selection in certain situations, based on the above diagnostics, to achieve maximum diversity and build diversity-interaction skills (an important future skill)
- Full-time, part-time, and self-pacing (not everyone in a unit must finish at the same time, but obviously group experiences would finish together)
- F2F experiences may be short-format (e.g. for corporate execs who travel in for a long-weekend experience once a month or for one week a quarter) or extended (e.g. teamwork during new-venture building). F2F experiences could be attended by learners who know each other and are in a degree journey together (a cohort) or include some attendees who are joining only that particular workshop or unit
- Online, searchable alumni and corporate-ecosystem platform
- Ability to earn "points" as a coach or mentor, to redeem for units, certifications, events, projects, etc. (i.e. a learning ecosystem marketplace). Since the best way to learn is to teach, this would be especially encouraged for all learners as a next step beyond mastery of particular skills/attributes
- Pre-program job placement (larger companies can do this, especially those that already have integrated work/learn entry programs)
- Business-outcome reporting for open innovation and consulting projects

A learning loop (otherwise known as "research") should be embedded into the process – tracking which elements of pre-admission testing and program performance are actually correlated with each other and learner goals such as placements, career performance, and new venture success.

Overall, a one-year program that features certification from a variety of big-brand schools, plus an incubator-like experience should prove attractive to budding entrepreneurs. With 600 million of them in the world in 2023 (about 7.4% of the population), the total addressable market is big. Since that number increased by 2.1% since 2020, it appears to be a growing market, too.

Since the year would feature multiple learn-do-reflect cycles in the process of developing a product/service/venture, learners would have more to show for their efforts than self-development. At the end of the program, they would have big-brand certifications useful for job advancement/placement, new skills, and a new product/service/venture to launch.

How to Disrupt: Examples to Build On

It's great to have a future vision, but focusing, launching, and growing an offering and its enterprise are essential to making it real. Below are a few examples of organizations that have shaken up industries or created new ones (i.e. disruptors), along with key lessons for you while you build your educational future.

Cirque du Soleil: Think Deeply about Needs

A creative band of street performers gathered feedback from audience members in a dying industry – the circus – and got sadly negative results. They didn't stop there and move on, though. They asked what people really want from a performance and dug into what people get from ballet, cabaret, music concerts (including opera), theatre, and of course, street performance.

What they found led them to integrate the best of different genres and launch a new category of entertainment – the theme show. Part circus, part ballet, part theatre, part musical, and more, their shows feature brilliant acrobatics, costuming, dance, lighting, music, staging, and stories. "We Reinvent the Circus" was one of their first shows.

Today, they earn $850 million–$1 billion annually and are the world's largest contemporary circus provider, valued at $1.5 billion. Across 300 cities on six continents, they've entertained nearly 150 million people (Meadows, 2021).

Look at an industry ripe for disruption (like education) as an opportunity. Start with what people need and want. Learn from best practices in analogous situations, e.g. other industries or other situations in customers' lives. Put the ingredients together, stir, and bake something new.

IBM, MetLife, and LumenLab: Spinning Off Disruptions

IBM is one of the few tech firms in the world that has lasted over a century (others include Nokia, NEC, and HP).

How did they do it?

When faced with new technologies to sell, requiring radically different resources, processes, and profit formulas, IBM spun off the business and let them operate independently – yet allowing them to use the much-trusted IBM brand name. Mainframes, for example, sold for millions and required custom design, long sales cycles, and a highly qualified sales team in traditional IBM-blue suits. When minicomputers came along at much cheaper prices, more-standard offerings (some customization needed), short sales cycles, and SME-friendly salespeople in business casual were needed. PCs were offered at even lower prices as standard products, and you could pick one up in a store in ten minutes from a blue-jeans-clad salesperson. Same brand, different businesses.

Further, although companies do not generally disrupt themselves, they can host disruptive innovation teams. At LumenLab for example (part of MetLife), problems and opportunities arise from the existing business and from the innovation team itself. The team works on it, and if the solution they come up with is sustaining (helps today's business), they roll it out in the business. If the solution is disruptive, they spin it off into a new venture, with the existing business' resources at hand, as needed (like marketing and distribution channels, a customer base, experts, data, etc.).

Consider using this approach in your own school or your investee schools.

Open Innovation: Best of Old and New

Incumbent companies are criticized for not being innovative enough, but the truth is, they innovate all the time. New products and services are regularly released, including new and improved versions of old ones. The business itself undergoes changes to improve how it operates. Incumbents have funding for innovation, patents and technologies, a customer base, supply chain, a trust-inducing brand (hopefully), and more. But they are generally slow, bureaucratic, cautious, and uncomfortable with pivots, which are essential when innovating something genuinely new or radically different.

Start-ups are the opposite. They don't have the resources, but they're fast, nimble, pivot-friendly, creative, and more.

Open innovation is a way for corporates and start-ups to work together to blend (hopefully) the best of both. Start-ups are sourced from the world's pool of teams already working on a given problem, they work together on agreed challenges, and at the end of the process, what comes out might be adopted into the product/service lines of the incumbent, launch as an incumbent-funded start-up, or make an impact in other ways.

If you're thinking your own organization will never be able to innovate something radically new and better than what you're doing today, learn more about open innovation and consider doing it. Some of the world's top companies are happy with the results.

Retailing: Why Not Brick-and-Click Education?

When eCommerce first came out, retailers were so scared that online shopping would take over their landscape. And yet here we are, decades later, with stores everywhere. In developing eBusinesses, we learned that "click" shopping offers broad selections, convenient ordering, often-better pricing, and more. However, some people simply enjoy shopping, do it as a social experience, want advice on what to buy, and want to try things out F2F (sound a little like education?).

What we learned is that neither one really wins. The most effective model was not "brick" or "click" but rather "brick-and-click" – an integration of the best features of the two. We also learned that holding both traditional businesses and new ones can be an effective approach as traditional businesses recraft themselves (and may shrink) and new businesses evolve (and hopefully grow).

Consider whether your education services would be better brick-and-click, mixing the best of online and F2F. You might be surprised by what you design and how your stakeholders – learners, parents, teachers, corporate recruiters, and others – react.

Uber and Airbnb: Why Not Uberize Education?

Uber, Grab, Gojek, and other ride-hailing services have done well. And yet we still have profitable taxi drivers, many of whom turn off their meters to take hailed rides before returning to their taxi-company rides. Airbnb has grown immensely, and yet we still have hotels. The market itself has grown, with the pricing and expanded range of the newcomers, but there must be more to the story of why they still co-exist.

Will taxis and hotels disappear? It's anyone's guess, but for now, they fill different needs, offer expanded choices, and there's probably a place for both.

Does this say something about education? I think so. There's room for older players and newer players (or designs), and there's surely room for a certain degree of collaboration or at least co-existence.

As our learners show us, humans and our organizations are nothing, if not adaptable, and there are probably "sharing economy" models of education to explore. The global educational platform mentioned above and the mixing of EdX and Coursera courses into established-school curricula show us that.

Does it mean individuals (like Uber drivers or Airbnb hosts) will begin offering their own learning journeys on an educational platform, just as institutions do, borrowing ratings and feedback systems from ride hailing and rental hosting?

Perhaps someone should launch that platform and see.

WeDoctor: Healthcare Gets an Amazon – How About Education?

WeDoctor is China's largest digital healthcare platform. It links doctors and hospitals with patients, insurers, financial services institutions, and pharmacies for online physician consultations, diagnostics, prescription filling, and more. Founded in 2010, it grew to 100 million users by 2016 and 250 million by 2022. In 2019, it earned $77 billion.

For too many years, healthcare has been a fragmented situation, and it sometimes takes more time and energy to manage the patient-journey than the underlying illness. Sadly, some cancer patients choose to forego chemotherapy not only because they don't want to repeat the agonizing process but also because they don't want to incur the paperwork and financial burden again.

Does this sound a little like education? Fragmented offerings, scattered (and different) entry requirements, paperwork hassle, financial burdens? If you're an investor or entrepreneur, you might consider launching or investing in an educational platform like WeDoctor that makes educational life smoother and more manageable. (Sorry – the name WeLearn's already taken, although you can investigate where it's registered and whether WeLearn would license the name.)

What About Accreditation?

As part of an institution launching and running accredited programs, I've been shocked by the manpower and resources (time included) required by the accreditation process. It not only covers program design and delivery but all aspects of the organization, itself, from structure and financial stability to policies and procedures to faculty qualifications, and beyond.

Today's accreditation system would be a burden – probably an unworkable one (unless it, too, is transformed) for new, nimble offerings. Start-ups can't wait a year after design for approval of a new offering. That said, executive education and giving a certificate of participation doesn't require accreditation (some incubators also do this). If people find value in the offering, they'll do it, and an accredited version can be offered later.

That said, customers do need some assurance of quality, unless the organization is operating under a currently recognized brand name – but beware – the organization's brand police may impose their own daunting quality checks and process.

How might we assure quality without destroying innovators? Ratings and reviews work well for products and services – not only for consumers but even for potential employees (e.g. Glassdoor). Building and managing brands is, actually, another quality-assurance process and way of communicating it.

After all, when Harvard offers executive education, does anyone care if it's accredited?

Certification is another approach. While accreditation focuses on ensuring the learning process and outcomes, certifications just focus on outcomes. When I took the CPA exam, for example, no one cared how I learned – just that I did learn and could perform to established standards.

Perhaps a new accreditation body and techniques are needed. Since disruption normally addresses the bottom of the market, new accreditors will likely be brand-name organizations that want to promote education for economic development. These may include:

- World Bank
- Asian Development Bank
- Gates Foundation
- Rockefeller Foundation
- UNDP
- Etc.

Although the abovementioned organizations are all well-respected, they are also known for bureaucracy. It will be essential that a disruptive accreditation body itself be a disruptive start-up with new operations and processes unshackled by the bureaucracy of its funding organizations. It can be part of the organization's portfolio and use the brand name, but like IBM's successive spin-offs, it would need to operate as a separate business.

Three Options for Launch and Growth

Based on all the needs, business models, and technologies described above, educators and investors face not only a choice of what to create, but also the approach for launch and growth. Thee three basic approaches to choose from include:

- **Big Bang** (lead the industry) – build everything, likely to involve acquisitions
- **Middle of the Road** (be a key player) – build part of the vision and use what can be adapted in the existing school, growing into the full vision later
- **Disruptor/Start-up** (be a disruptor) – start small, experiment with inexpensive offerings for the bottom of the market (or customers currently excluded – those not even in the market), and when you have something profitable, scale quickly

The disruptor/start-up model involves less risk of wasting money by building the wrong thing (since you start small and experiment), but it does pose the risk that someone will launch the next educational Uber/Airbnb/Amazon first, overtaking your position with no chance for you to catch up.

The reason funders were so patient with Amazon's lack of profitability for so long was because, for a platform venture, the first one to dominate the market generally wins. However, if you don't intend to launch a platform, being a disruptor is a good approach.

That said, first-mover advantage doesn't always happen. Some funders pursue the second mover after the first mover has invested in crafting the offering and made the mistakes. The second one aims to leapfrog and do it better.

After all, McDonald's used to spend millions every year researching locations on which to place restaurants. (Perhaps it still does.)

Burger King just opens across the street.

The Dream Team

If you go the disruptor route, the leadership team – including board composition and advisory board membership – matters. Obviously, it should be an innovative, diverse team including different industry experience, fields, nationalities, psychological style, genders, ages, backgrounds, and any other useful diversity you can think of (e.g. neurodiversity).

Whom would I like to invite to a team, board, and advisory board for a global, hybrid, K-12 school? Ricardo Semler, Sal Kahn, founder of Gojek and Indonesian Minister of Education Nadiem Makarim, unschooling parent and artist from Woodstock KK Raghava (who's also a multi-TED speaker), Peggy Rockefeller Dulaney from Synergos, Gates and Rockefeller Foundations, Tim Brown from IDEO, Sam Altman from open.ai, B20 speaker and start-up advisor/investor Paul Bradley, a technologist from squirrel.ai, Jack Sim, celebrity chef Ryan Clift, (who dropped out of school at 13 to work in a Michelin-star restaurant), Gnowbe founder So-Young Kang, Google L&D designer Sarah Brown, positive psychologist Tal Ben-Shahar, and others, including learners, parents, educators, and community representatives.

Yes, yes, I know, but I did say it's a "dream" team.

Recommendations for Students, Educators, and Investors

Students

Although you're not enrolling in the vision, there are elements of it already out there. Stop and think before you pursue a standard offering that may not be right for you or may be more expensive than you need. Read through the vision and consider how you might bring elements of it into your own life and education, where appropriate.

Know that life experience is something to design, too – another form of the "bucket list". Remember you may get "credit" for it, too, depending on what formal program you may join. Actively build your learning community (including joining one(s) that already exist). You'll reap benefits over your whole life from building a unique – maybe even quirky and eclectic – social network. Use them and remember to contribute to the learning and work of others in your network. It'll come back to you when you least expect it.

Bottom line: you can take charge of your own education – and its cost – like never before.

Educators

As the industry matures and is disrupted, and as offerings become more modular (e.g. "plug and play" courses like Harvard Online's CoRe), you'll need to shift from a one-stop-shop strategy to a modular strategy, competing on the basis of specific offerings. You should consider whether different elements of your business should be disintegrated or "unpacked" and further modularized and specialized.

Read through the vision and consider if any elements are needed by your stakeholders – learners, parents, teachers, tutors, community. Will the elements make your existing school better? Incorporate them. Will they threaten your school, but they're needed? Spin them out.

Can you try out one program quickly, experiment, and build on it? Don't launch it right away. Investigate needs in a design-thinking manner. Dream and design with wild ideas (you can bring them down later if needed). Prototype and experiment before launching. There are lots of resources for learning and trying out this approach on the Design Thinking tab of my website. It's there for you to use.

Consider launching non-accredited offerings for truly unmet needs. People who've already fallen out of the "system" have nothing. Anything useful is better. You can go through accreditation later if needed.

Whatever you decide to do, remember to gather data on how your newly launched offering works and the results, so you can evaluate and evolve your emergent strategy.

Remember not to do it alone. Who's your dream team? Bring them into your process to help with inputs and ideas, access, feedback on your designs, and anything else they're happy to offer. It's surprising how happy to help many people are. People like to be part of something bigger and longer-lasting than themselves.

After all, what could be bigger and more long-lasting than changing the foundation of people's lives – how and what they learn?

Investors

Remember that as industries mature (e.g. education) and "interfaces" become more standard (e.g. "plug and play" courses like Harvard Online's CoRe), businesses need to shift from a one-stop-shop strategy to a modular strategy, competing on the basis of specific offerings. You may see your established investees disintegrating (not necessarily disappearing). Help them rethink their integrated strategies and whether they need to disintegrate (not disappear), modularize, and specialize.

Trawl through the vision and decide if any elements would be a good fit for your investees. Approach them supportively. If you think a new wave of education will pass them by, consider whether you want to maintain your investment in them.

For your start-ups and particular offerings, are they radical enough? Have they included all relevant elements of the vision? What part will they play in tomorrow's education landscape? Who else should you look for (and maybe partner with) to round out your part of that landscape?

Guide them carefully while they – and you – consider the big bang, leading player, and disruptor approaches and journey to scale. It's beyond the scope of this book to give advice on each of those areas for your investee, but there are books, programs, coaches, mentors, and communities out there (TiE.org, for example) you can leverage.

Do impress upon your investees the need to gather data on how their newly launched offering works and the results, so they (and you) can evaluate and evolve their emergent strategy.

Don't forget to build your dream team. Not only can they help your individual portfolio companies, but they can also help across your portfolio, and you have the special perspective across your portfolio to have your investee companies help each other.

9 Conclusions, Insights, and Your Next Steps

Never look down to test the ground before taking your next step; only he who keeps his eyes fixed on the far horizon will find the right road.

–Dag Hammarskjöld, Former Secretary-General of the United Nations.

Pulling It All Together – Now

Feel the urgency.
Understand disruption.
Think like a designer.
Understand your "users" (and potential users') needs.
Develop people for the future.
Work in new ways with new business models.
Use technology effectively.
Craft your own vision.
Design, launch, and grow.

DOI: 10.4324/9781003340713-9

These are all my recommendations for you, and this book is intended to both inspire you and enable you to make it happen. You won't be the only future-builder, but I pray you're one of them and that there are a lot of us.

Funny enough, disrupting, responding to disruption, and Design Thinking are not only useful for education, but they're skillsets you need to learn and help others learn, for whatever future we build.

In an AI-enabled world, human skills like choosing and framing challenges, finding needs, investigating unstructured situations without much (or any) data, asking good questions, uncovering information and understanding people with empathy, generating deeper insights, using creative and critical thinking skills together to envision the future, designing the new, prototyping and experimenting, and entrepreneurially launching and growing the new are all needed. And they're all very human.

The future of work for humans will focus on these sorts of activities our advanced technologies are not good at.

What we do will change, how we do it, and of course, what and how we learn.

Finally, Some Thoughts for Policymakers

I haven't addressed policymakers yet in this book because – my apologies – I am biased against big-government welfare-state-style provision of services. Frankly, I'm not alone.

That said, surely governments can operate in new ways or at least take action without taking over.

Government departments are (in general) big, incumbent organizations that don't face disruption and displacement the same way corporations do.

So, disruption has nothing to do with government, right?

Wrong.

Clay Christen was shocked one day when a phone call came in from the US Department of Defense. They wanted to learn about disruption theory from the man who created it.

Why?

He asked them that very question, and they reminded him what disruptors are like: small teams, new and nimble organizations, advanced technologies, not playing by the "rules of the game". They asked him what military-relevant organizations that could describe.

Terrorists.

For a big, incumbent defense department to respond to terrorist-disruptors, they needed to think like them and operate like them.

Disruption is not just a challenge for defense, it's also relevant to economic growth – both economic activity and the education system that produces people who grow the economy.

Is there a small, nimble government that advises big players like China?

Yes.

Singapore.

The nation-state housing only 6 million residents grew its per-capita GDP from $472 in 1962 to almost $83,000 in 2022 – just 60 years (World Bank, as cited in Macrotrends, 2024). Its current per-capita GDP is nearly $92,000 (IMF, 2024), and in adjusted terms, it's second in the world (after Luxembourg), ahead of the UAE, UK, and US (Worlddata.info, 2024).

Small, nimble, fast-acting players do have something to teach the rest of us, and even a government can be an effective socio-economic engineer without becoming a welfare state.

OK, then surely Design Thinking has nothing to do with government, right?

Wrong.

Design Thinking is used in governments around the world to provide better, faster, cheaper services. In Singapore, for example, when the Ministry of Manpower used a design-thinking approach for their Work Pass Division (WPD), services that used to take half a day of on-site waiting now take 90% of those served only ten minutes. WPD relocated to a smaller (less costly) service center, and operations are more efficient via streamlined, accurate processing, as well as more enjoyable, with play stations for children while they wait (less stress on the staff and "customers").

So, can governments take a disruption and Design Thinking approach – leveraging new designs, business models, and technologies – to economic growth and the necessary education to support it?

Yes.

Are any of them doing it now?

Yes.

Indonesia's president realized the nation needed a new way to do just that and invited the founder of $10 billion transportation company Gojek to become the new Minister of Education. But it takes more than one person to make change. Nadiem Makarim is not a lone wolf trying to revolutionize the nation's education system on his own.

He recruited a 400-person team of young unicorn techies – people who never would have considered working for government before the new initiative – to infuse the government ministry with new ideas and approaches. Not only are they there to make education better for the future – they're also there to make government operate more like a big start-up.

Their education system has already seen a shift from knowledge testing to application, problem-solving, and critical thinking, and 30% of the standard curriculum has been removed in favor of skills needed for the future of work in the future economy. Teachers now connect with each other through tech and learn from each other as a community, for continuous improvement.

I won't repeat here the B20/G20 recommendations (2023), including digital literacy in schools, digital access (especially for underprivileged groups), skills forecasting, educational support, digital skills libraries/central training materials, and more. The report is freely available on the Internet.

However, I would like to share some of what other governments are doing, to give you a flavor of what's happening and a little fear of missing out (FOMO). You may also like to contact officials in the below-named governments to find out more about their journeys and what various organizations they work with can do for you.

To support their future economies, Germany and Italy use skills surveys, assessments, forecasts, and employer-employee research to generate useful data so policymakers, employers, citizens, and educators can make data-based decisions. They generate job market projections, and the analysis feeds into policymaking. The European Center for the Development of Vocational Training (CEDEFOP) mines online job vacancies (OJVs) and conducts the European skills and jobs survey and the European skills forecast to produce the European skills index and try to anticipate skills needed in the marketplace.

Other governments also use skills frameworks and projections at an aggregate level, but with new technologies, it's possible to drill down to individual employers and employees. Epitome does this and has been hired by the government of Mexico and others for their data-gathering and analytics at a national level, as well as to give recommendations to individual citizens on skills they could seek for particular jobs open now or forecast in the future.

India Skills Report also takes an integrated economy-education approach. Via the Wheebox National Employability Test (WNET), India Hiring Intent Survey, and inputs from 152 corporations across 15 industries, it provides a comprehensive analysis of job demand and talent supply in various states across the nation. It also highlights work trends shared by leaders in both academia and industry.

Remember: in an age where computers can increasingly code themselves and our tools become stunningly user-friendly, you should question your survey results indicating demand for growing numbers of coders in particular languages and technologists using today's interfaces. Remind your readers (and other users of your data) that questioning, thinking, learning, interacting effectively, and above all adaptability should be top-of-mind for education designers, employers, and learners.

In Australia, the Skills Matching and Jobseeker Support (SMJS) program provides job seekers with personalized job search assistance and support, and the Higher Education Loan Programme (HELP) provides income-contingent loans for higher education. The EU's DigComp framework outlines digital competencies needed for the increasingly digital economy and society, including benchmarks that are integrated into national policies and strategies for digital skills development. It also serves as a framework for companies to evaluate the digital competencies of their workforce.

In Singapore, SkillsFuture promotes lifelong learning and career development for a future-ready Singapore and provides SkillsFuture Credits to fund up to 90% of approved courses. Every citizen over 25 years of age receives $370 for learning inside or outside their field. Those over 40 receive nearly $3,000 for approved courses. For prison inmates, university tuition is subsidized up to 100% upon re-entry into society. In France, the Compte Personnel de Formation (CPF) provides annual training funds to all employees – $870 for unskilled workers, and $550 for full-time, skilled workers.

Nations like Australia, Brazil, China, Germany, India, Japan, South Africa, Spain, the UK, and the US have all done their homework and forecast an onslaught of needs in the green economy, healthcare, cybersecurity, and more – including more jobs in education to skill new workers.

That said, there's a catch (there always is).

Funding lifelong and career learning for the future economy is a good idea, but it has its dark side. With a Harvard doctorate and decades of experience leading workshops and designing learning programs, I'm not actually qualified to teach courses in some government schemes. I would have to take scheme-based training and certification to teach, and the mediocre potential compensation has never induced me into their programs.

Further, I did offer a half-day course through a partner (so we got around the teaching restriction with a qualified partner and one-off approval). Not only did it take six months to get approval for the workshop (and that was fast-tracked!), but there were certain restrictions. My half-day course couldn't actually be four hours because there had to be a 45-minute test at the end, comprising multiple choice, short answer, and a case essay based on a custom-written case (by me). OK, we got through that, and then I was told the 15-minute tea break couldn't be held when I wanted to because it was a good breaking point for the work we were doing. It had to be held at 10:45 am.

What was the course about?

Creativity.

I understand the need to verify that people aren't taking advantage of government generosity, but in the race to structure and certify, we can easily overdo it. Just be vigilant when you're overseeing policies and programs – not so much against being taken advantage of, but against your own over-vigilance.

In fact, take a Design Thinking approach (of course) and see how your policies and programs are working in real life – by being there, grass-roots-level.

Reality might shock you.

One reality that has shocked governments is the plethora of people **not** taking advantage of government's extensive analysis and skills funding.

For example, although the EU administration aims to make lifelong learning a universal right, only 10% of adults participate in training, with less qualified and unemployed workers being the **least** trained. OECD countries are doing better, but still not enough to reskill and upskill for the digital future.

Only about 40% of adults participate in job-related training annually, and most of these are from the highly skilled workforce. Adult learning among lower-skilled workers sits at just over 20% (B20, 2023, p. 56).

Given the predictions of reskilling needed in the age of AI, perhaps we'll see those numbers improve in the face of unemployment for those who don't enhance their skills. Or perhaps something beyond economic need is keeping learners away.

It's worth investigating.

Whatever the problems, and given the need to design for them, most educators agree that established institutions have been slow to revamp what they do. Most predict the rise of alternative education. Policymakers can help that rise with recognition of new programs and skills (without over-certifying everything), funding for innovators (new education ventures that also grow the economy), and funding for consumers of education.

At the K-12 level in the US, such support initiated the school voucher debate. I'm not going to dig into the pros and cons here beyond highlighting some issues relevant to K-12, higher education, and lifelong learning.

The basic idea of school vouchers is that if schools are not serving students well, and private education is pursued, it's not fair to levy taxes on parents who don't use the school and also have to pay for another school.

Fair enough.

On the other hand, the US school system alone educates 50 million students. Any innovation rolled out there would have a huge impact. Further, giving vouchers, tuition tax credits (for individuals and companies that donate to scholarship-granting institutions), and low-tax education savings accounts draws financial support from the institutions that serve not only a mass market of learners but especially serves the ones at the bottom of the market who couldn't even consider private education. Choices between schools are given in many jurisdictions, but then there's the problem of over-enrollment, competition, travel to far-way schools, etc.

For uni, the US government takes part in loan funding, but in the EU, the voucher debate is relevant, since uni is partially or fully funded in many locations.

I think it's fair to say that the existing institutions will remain, but we need to open up the "market" to new, innovative players. Like the Uber and Airbnb example earlier, there's room for the old and new, and there should be opportunities for new education providers to operate as "plug-ins", or for the old institutions to decouple place and program, operating as WeLearns.

AI-enabled, personalized curricula and tools could make schools into learning centers, not just one-size-fits-all education providers. Government can provide funding for the place(s), program(s), or (probably) both in newer, more flexible ways.

It's a revolutionary idea – schools (including uni) that house but don't (always) teach – but it may be a welcomed option for those who want a social learning space, a learning community (not just employed teachers and paying students), and also want to choose their learning from the best the global marketplace has to offer.

Policymakers can also invite companies to the table so policymakers, educators, and businesses can collaborate and design together.

My basic message is this: get disruptive – something you may have thought didn't apply to you.

Learn from analogous situations (a Design Thinking practice), e.g. India's Nanda Nilhakani, who spearheaded the national ID system with fingerprint and iris-scan technology – the most advanced in the world. An old way of doing things, managed by the government, was replaced nationwide at start-up speed. In just eight years, the voluntary program collected iris scans, fingerprints, and photos of over 1.2 billion people. It has also enabled non-government activities to flourish, e.g. small-business loan programs for job-rich economic growth.

Foster an educational ecosystem the way governments foster innovation ecosystems. Policymakers don't dictate how start-ups work, but they do provide infrastructure, programs, and incentives that help. Support (including financially) grassroots initiatives, instead of only the big players and the existing "system".

Next Steps for Investors, Educators, Employers, and Students

> It was 1999 – 25 years ago. That week of sharing knowledge (at the Oberoi summer university) had such a profound influence on me that I took a sabbatical and did my master's in business. I came back to India so full of confidence to start my own business that when I met Mr. Oberoi to see if I should resume my duties post-sabbatical, I gave him my resignation – just like that (and without thinking about it beforehand!). When I reached home, my family was shocked that I took this maverick step without anything in hand. I had spent all the money I had saved on the course, so basically, I was starting out with nothing.
>
> It's been a roller coaster of a ride since 2002. I founded a one-man consultancy to make sure there was food on the table, as well as other enterprises. After a painful rebuild post-2008-crisis, I co-founded an eCommerce company called Licious. We are nine years old, based in Bangalore, and own the entire supply chain from farm to customer doorstep. We employ around 4,500 superheroes across India and are present in 26 cities – and still growing.
>
> Our last round of funding was at a valuation of $1.6 billion. I write this not to impress you but to impress upon you the importance of researching, the profound influence of a handful of people on my thinking, the importance of taking time out to understand a business more deeply, the need to develop rich personal networks, and facing the fear of failure with action.
>
> –Joe Manavalan, Unicorn Founder

I won't repeat here what you can see in the "Recommendations for" section at the end of each of the above chapters. Instead, I'll just say: **now's your time to shift from being reactive to proactive, from being problem-focused to vision-focused, and from seeing parts to seeing wholes.**

It's time to disrupt, design, launch, and grow.

Investors

Disruption theory's creator Clay Christensen didn't just write books. He founded a consulting firm (Innosight) to help people turn their ideas into realities. He also founded an investment fund to analyze and invest in startups who looked like they would be winners in disruptive situations. Backed by research-based analysis, the last I heard, it was making very outsized returns.

Outsized returns can also be found in design-focused organizations, which have been extensively researched. You can look for design leadership, practices, and culture in your future investees and encourage them in your current investees, if you want:

- **Up to twice the industry-average growth and 75% higher shareholder returns** (Sheppard et al., 2018, describing the top 25% of Design Index score companies)
- **Faster operating income growth** (up to three times as fast as peers), double Return on Assets, and 60% more shareholder returns by directly capturing customer insights, instead of capturing the latest industry trends report (Strategy&, as quoted in Jaruzelski et al., 2014)
- **Outperformance of the S&P index by 228%** and the **FTSE 100 by 231%** for 10 consecutive years (Westcott et al., 2013)

Next steps (after reviewing all the recommendations sections above): talk with your investees about how to incorporate disruption and Design Thinking, as well as new needs, business, models, and tech. Rethink their integrated strategies vs. disintegrated, modular, specialist strategies.

Be skeptical of long-term programs in technical skills we're forecast to need. By the time learners have learned, there may be AI interfaces making their skills obsolete. Remember the need for questioning, thinking, learning, interacting effectively, and above all, adaptability.

Check out government forecasts and incentives. You may want to take advantage of some. Talk to your co-funders about hunting for new investees with these lenses.

Educational Institution Leaders

Besides understanding that you will be disrupted and the speed at which it will probably happen (once it starts in earnest), learn Design Thinking (if you haven't already) and apply it. Go through the recommendations in the chapters in this book and consult with your leadership team, learners, parents, hiring companies, community, and investors. Consult the skills-future studies your government produces and talk with policymakers about the support they offer and the support you'd like them to offer.

There's a lot we can do now without changing the regulatory framework. Homeschooling is already legal and on the rise; universities already offer credits for work experience; and people already study on their own for various certifications (e.g. IGCSEs, A-levels, CPA, bar exams, corporate certifications, etc.). There's no need to completely throw out the old in favor of the new if we can keep the old elements that'll serve us well in the future and integrate them with the new.

We only have to throw out the old if it won't adapt.

The last thing you'll want to do is take on too much, but the last-last thing you'll want to do (is that a thing?) is do nothing. Build your own vision with your stakeholders, your own strategy, your own implementation approach, and a "learning loop", whereby you gather data on what you've done and how well or poorly it's performed, then adjust your strategy.

Frankly, you'll gather data on how well **and** poorly your initiatives have performed. Don't be discouraged. Expect it. Be excited, use the feedback, and make something better.

If you're a new venture, know that you're competing against accredited players with existing brand names. Partner with existing educators and build your ecosystem of old and new players.

If you're an incumbent, consider open innovation, participate in marketplaces, partner, and adapt to the new.

And, of course, when designing your offerings on the basis of skills forecasts, ensure that any technical skills you're offering are in short-term programs, because AI interfaces (e.g. self-coding software) are quickly making today's skills obsolete. Remember the need for questioning, thinking, learning, interacting effectively, and adaptability.

Front-Line Educators (Including Parents)

First, start using tech (e.g. ChatGPT) to make your job easier in any way it can. Take a lesson from the guy who outsourced himself. He hired a worker in India to do his job and paid him a fraction of his own salary. Feedback started coming back on how much his work had improved – even social parts of the job like the tone and responsiveness of his emails. He spent his new leisure time on other pursuits. (I think cat videos and hobbies were involved.)

Sadly, he was fired for giving unauthorized access to company systems to an outsider (so don't do exactly as he did). Nonetheless, wherever possible, have technology be your outsourced employee and spend your time doing and improving the human parts of your job.

Ask yourself, "why was I hired into this job?". Understand what you're needed for and what you want. Use psychometrics or at least self-reflection to pursue the parts you want to. Partner effectively with others to provide what you don't want to. Build your ecosystem.

Use the Design Thinking and disruption lenses to design or improve your offerings. Like your students, who'll have to figure out how they're designed and then operate in a world where old jobs die and new ones are born, seek needs, design how you'll fulfill them, prototype, and launch what you do into the marketplace, whether it's a real marketplace, the marketplace inside your organization, or the marketplace of activities you and your homeschoolers choose from.

Your organization may say no, they don't want your new offerings. If you don't find the reasons valid, consider changing to a more innovative employer or becoming a start-up, yourself.

If you're teaching people in long-term technical programs or are a concerned parent reading government forecasts of the growth of technology-based careers, remember that AI interfaces are already changing the tech-skill landscape and will continue to do so. Software can code itself to some extent today, and that trend will continue. Remember the value of questioning, thinking, learning, interacting effectively, and adaptability.

Employers

Leverage forecasts and tools (e.g. Deloitte's Future of Work forecaster and Epitome) not only to understand your workforce today, but to envision in detail the workforce you're going to need in the next five years. Don't imagine you can just replace every worker or that they'll all create and perform in the digital future with no learning today. We all need new skills for a new world of work. Plan your skilling, reskilling, and upskilling programs.

That said, be skeptical about forecasts for particular technological skills for today's technology interfaces. AI will layer over much of that and transform what we do, making some of those skills rapidly obsolete. Remember that you'll need (even more than before) skills in questioning, thinking, learning, interacting effectively, and above all adaptability.

Have a conversation with policymakers about what you're seeing in your own workforce and how policymakers are planning to support employers like you. Take advantage of whatever support is appropriate for you.

Invite educational institutions to co-create what you need. Strategic learning particular to you will remain inside you. The rest should be released into the marketplace, possibly using your brand, thereby spreading and strengthening it. Your co-creation agreement should specify profit-sharing or royalties, as well as branding. Employers today have been operating as educators for a long time and have already released their training into the marketplace via Coursera, Gnowbe, Credly, and others. (IBM certifications, for example, are popular.)

Don't be shy about using what's on these platforms, either. Remember that strategic learning should be part of your operations. Non-strategic should be outsourced.

If you hire from educational institutions, make sure you have a seat at the table designing and updating what they deliver, so you don't have to retrain workers who've supposedly already been trained.

Students

You'll be pretty busy with the recommendations at the end of each chapter above. The only thing to add to it is to be happy that you're learning and working in a time of great change. That may sound crazy, but think about it. Would you rather decide when you're 16 who you're going to be, mold yourself into that role and persona, then pursue a career in it for the next 40 years whether your decision was right or wrong?

The average person now changes jobs every 2.75 years and has three to seven careers before retiring (if that's even a "thing", anymore). Gen-Z can apparently expect to hold 16–17 jobs across five to seven careers (UQ, 2023).

Since I come from a self-pay education nation (the US), my bias was always for get-a-job degrees (accounting, in my case). I'm now far more open-minded about learn-how-to-think degrees like those you find in liberal arts programs. Not only did I discover that places like Accenture would hire French and English literature majors and then train them how to code computer software (they wanted people who could think, learn, and adapt), but the work we'll do should change dramatically in our lifetime. AI will take over some of what we do, but you'll need (even more than before) skills in **questioning, thinking, learning, interacting effectively, and above all adaptability.**

So, begin with a growth mindset and never let go of it; reflect often (annually is good for major life/work reflection); write letters to your past self (Jeff Bezos wrote a great one a couple of years ago); build your ecosystem (including mentors and maybe a personal board of directors); expect lifelong learning; and craft your own work and learning path with:

- What's in the global marketplace
- Government support
- Work and volunteering
- World travel (there are work programs in homes as caretakers or au pairs and work programs on farms like WWOOF that help you support a global journey)
- Your own designs (which you might then offer to others)

Enjoy.

That's important.

We have do-overs in life, but the clock ticks only one way as you do.

Final Thoughts

I can't wait to see what future you create for yourself and others!

Connect and collaborate.

With this book and its companion Gnowbe "living book" (multimedia content + action prompts + community), you're invited to a dialogue (a multilogue, actually) and can reach out easily for discussion and collaboration.

Let's build the future together.

Bibliography

Ackoff, R., & Greenberg, D. (2008). *Turning learning right side up: Putting education back on track.* Wharton School Publishing.

Anonymous. (2023, November 28). Personal interview with IDC researcher.

AwakenFutures (part of Awaken Group). (2023). *Future of education 2030.* AwakenFutures.

B20. (2023). *Task force on future of work, skilling, and mobility policy paper.* Confederation of Indian Industry (CII).

Bersin, J., & Zao-Sanders, M. (2019, February 19). Making learning a part of everyday work. *Harvard Business Review Online.* https://hbr.org/2019/02/making-learning-a-part-of-everyday-work

Bradley, P. (2023, March). Personal interview and speech at the B20/G20 CII Partnership Summit, Delhi, India. https://www.youtube.com/watch?v=EluVf5KMufY

Brodnitz, D. (2024, February 28). The most in-demand skills for 2024. *LinkedIn Learning.* https://www.linkedin.com/business/talent/blog/talent-strategy/linkedin-most-in-demand-hard-and-soft-skills

Brown, T. (2008). Design thinking. *Harvard Business Review.* https://hbr.org/

Casey, V. (2016, December 12). *Why can people get access to mobile phones, and not safe water?* [Blog post]. http://www.wateraid.org/news/blogs/2016/october/why-can-people-get-access-to-mobile-phones-and-not-safe-water

Christensen, C., Johnson, C., & Horn, M. (2010). *Disrupting class, expanded edition: How disruptive innovation will change the way the world learns* (2nd ed.). McGraw Hill.

DeMatteo, M. (2020, November 25). This is the average age when people finally pay off their student loans for good. *CNBC*. https://www.cnbc.com/select/how-long-it-takes-to-pay-off-student-loans/

Does Gamified Training Get Results? (2023, March–April). *Harvard Business Review*. https://hbr.org/2023/03/does-gamified-training-get-results

Duarte, F. (2023, November 3). Number of ChatGPT users. *Exploding Topics*. https://explodingtopics.com/blog/chatgpt-users

Economic Times. (2023). *ET conversations with OpenAI CEO Sam Altman*. https://www.youtube.com/watch?v=AiE7FsdRzz8

Fitzgerald, J. (2021, October 26). *HBS working knowledge, research & ideas section*. https://hbswk.hbs.edu/item/what-companies-want-most-in-a-ceo-a-good-listener

Flatt, J. (2008). *Loreto day school sealdah: Meeting the challenges of changing India*. A.J. Flatt.

Garelli, S. (2016). *Why you will probably live longer than most big companies*. IMD Research and Knowledge. https://www.imd.org/research-knowledge/disruption/articles/why-you-will-probably-live-longer-than-most-big-companies/

Hamelin, N., & Bonelli, M. (2022). Traders' anticipatory feelings and traders' profitability: An exploratory study. *Journal of Behavioral and Experimental Finance*, *36*, 100743.

Hamelin, N., Thaichon, P., Abraham, C., Driver, N., Lipscombe, J., & Pillai, J. (2020). Storytelling, the scale of persuasion and retention: A neuromarketing approach. *Journal of Retailing and Consumer Services*, *55*, 102099.

Hanauer, N. (2014). *Beware, fellow plutocrats, the pitchforks are coming* [Video]. http://www.ted.com/talks/nick_hanauer_beware_fellow_plutocrats_the_pitchforks_are_coming

Hanson, M. (2023, September 25). Average time to repay student loans. *EducationData.org*. https://educationdata.org/average-time-to-repay-student-loans

HBSP (Harvard Business School Publishing). (2023). *Transformative technologies: How analytics, AI, ChatGPT, and the metaverse are revolutionizing higher education*. HBS Press.

Horn, B., & Moesta, B. (2019, October 25). *Do colleges truly understand what students want from them?* https://hbsp.harvard.edu/do-colleges-truly-understand-what-students-want-from-them/

IDEO. (2014, July). *Designing a school system from the ground up*. https://www.ideo.com/work/designing-a-school-system

IMF (International Monetary Fund). (2024). *Singapore datasets*. https://www.imf.org/external/datamapper/profile/SGP

Iyer, P. (2013, July). *Where is home?* [Video]. https://www.ted.com/talks/pico_iyer_where_is_home

Jaruzelski, B., Staack, V., & Goehle, B. (2014). Proven paths to innovation success: Ten years of research reveal the best R&D strategies for the decade ahead. *Strategy + Business Magazine, 77*, 8.

Jebara, M. (2017). This company pays kids to do their math homework [Video]. *TED*. https://www.ted.com/talks/mohamad_jebara_this_company_pays_kids_to_do_their_math_homework?language=en

Kang, S. (2023, June). Personal interview with Awaken Group CEO.

Lodge, J. M., Howard, S., Bearman, M., Dawson, P., & Associates (2023). *Assessment reform for the age of artificial intelligence*. Tertiary Education Quality and Standards Agency (TEQSA).

Lumiar. (2016). *The school*. http://lumiar.org.br/index.php/a-escola/?lang=en

Macrotrends. (2024). *Singapore GDP Per Capita 1960-2024*. https://www.macrotrends.net/global-metrics/countries/SGP/singapore/gdp-per-capita

Manavalan, J. (2024, April 1–23). Personal communication.

Mcfeely, S., & Wigert, B. (2019, March 13). This fixable problem costs U.S. Businesses $1 Trillion. *Gallup Workplace*. https://www.gallup.com/workplace/247391/fixable-problem-costs-businesses-trillion.aspx

McGrath, R. (2013, November 25; updated 2019, September 25). The pace of technology adoption is speeding up. *Harvard Business Review Online*. https://hbr.org/2013/11/the-pace-of-technology-adoption-is-speeding-up

Meadows, C. (2020). *Innovation through fusion: Combining innovative ideas to create high-impact solutions*. De Gruyter.

Meadows, C. (2021). *Famous business fusions: Ideas that revolutionized industries*. De Gruyter.

Meléndez, C. (2022, February 17). Design thinking and data: The new power couple of 2022 [council post]. *Forbes Technology Council*. https://www.forbes.com/sites/forbestechcouncil/2022/02/17/designthinking-and-data-the-new-power-couple-of-2022/amp/

Mochari, I. (2016, March 23). Why half of the S&P 500 companies will be replaced in the next decade. *Inc*. https://www.inc.com/ilan-mochari/innosight-sp-500-new-companies.html

OpenAI. (2023). *ChatGPT (GPT4, Mar 14 version) [Large language model]*. https://chat.openai.com/chat

Pearson. (2014, January). *Index - Which countries have the best schools?* http://thelearningcurve.pearson.com/index/index-ranking

Perry, M. (2017, October 20). *Fortune 500 firms 1955 v. 2017: Only 60 remain, thanks to the creative destruction that fuels economic prosperity* [Blog post]. http://www.aei.org/publication/fortune-500-firms-1955-v-2017-only-12-remain-thanks-to-the-creative-destruction-that-fuels-economic-prosperity/

Radjou, N., Prabhu, J., & Ahuja, S. (2012). *Jugaad innovation: Think frugal, be flexible, generate breakthrough growth*. Jossey-Bass.

Semler, R. (2015, February). *How to run a company with (almost) no rules* [Video]. http://www.ted.com/talks/ricardo_semler_radical_wisdom_for_a_company_a_school_a_life

Sheppard, B., Kouyoumjian, G., Sarrazin, H., & Dore, F. (2018, October 25). The business value of design. *McKinsey Quarterly*. https://www.mckinsey.com/business-functions/mckinsey-design/our-insights/the-businessvalue-of-design

Sim, J. (2016, October 29). 7C's to survive an anti-jobs future. *Straits Times*. https://www.straitstimes.com/opinion/7cs-to-survive-an-anti-jobs-future

Standing, G. (2014). *The precariat: The new dangerous class*. Bloomsbury.

Stellar Market Research. (2021). *Asia pacific private tutorial market: Industry analysis and forecast (2024-2030)* (Report ID: SMR_967). https://www.stellarmr.com/report/Asia-Pacific-Private-Tutorial-Market/967#:~:text=Asia%20Pacific%20Private%20Tutorial%20Market%20was%20valued%20at%0USD%2044.79,8.4%25%20over%20the%20forecast%20period

Stetler, S. (2022, May). Want to advance in your career? Build your own board of directors. *Harvard Business Review Digital*. Product #: H071CQ-PDF-ENG

Traxler, C. R. (2015). The most democratic school of them all: Why the Sudbury model of education should be taken seriously. *Schools: Studies in Education, 12*(2), 271–296.

United Nations. (2023). *The sustainable development goals report: Special edition*. https://reliefweb.int/report/world/sustainable-development-goals-report-2023-special-edition?gad_source=1&gclid=CjwKCAjww_iwBhApEiwAuG6ccAw8K84yTvMXrMk9_a98CYl59fd7yCNDRCwlUt7_GEvaLBF5KPKlzRoCiwkQAvD_BwE

United Nations Department of Economic and Social Affairs. (2020). *World social report 2020: Inequality in a rapidly changing world*. United Nations. https://www.un.org/en/desa/world-social-report-2020#:~:text=The%20report%20found%20that%20inequalities,the%20needs%20of%20the%20majority.%E2%80%9D

University of Queensland. (2023, June 19). *How many career changes in a lifetime*. https://study.uq.edu.au/stories/how-many-career-changes-lifetime#:~:text=Research%20shows%20most%20people%20will,and%20upcoming%20generations%20of%20workers

Westcott, M., Sato, S., Mrazek, D., Wallace, R., Vanka, S., Bilson, C., & Hardin, D. (2013). The DMI design value scorecard: A new design measurement and management model. *Design Management Review, 24*(4), 10–16.

Wikipedia Contributors. (2016). *List of countries by GDP (PPP) per capita*. Wikipedia, The Free Encyclopedia. https://en.wikipedia.org/w/index.php?title=List_of_countries_by_GDP_(PPP)_per_capita&oldid=707650226

World Bank. (n.d.). *Small and Medium Enterprises (SMEs) finance*. https://www.worldbank.org/en/topic/smefinance

World Economic Forum. (2019). *The 10 skills you need to thrive in the fourth industrial revolution*. https://www.weforum.org/agenda/2016/01/the-10-skills-you-need-to-thrive-in-the-fourth-industrial-revolution/

Worlddata.info. (2024). *The 50 richest countries in the world*. https://www.worlddata.info/richest-countries.php

Index

For Product Safety Concerns and Information please contact our EU representative GPSR@taylorandfrancis.com
Taylor & Francis Verlag GmbH, Kaufingerstraße 24, 80331 München, Germany

www.ingramcontent.com/pod-product-compliance
Lightning Source LLC
LaVergne TN
LVHW010919110826
845149LV00013B/2422
9781032375434